T0248558

# Backpacking Florida

UNIVERSITY PRESS OF FLORIDA

Florida A&M University, Tallahassee
Florida Atlantic University, Boca Raton
Florida Gulf Coast University, Ft. Myers
Florida International University, Miami
Florida State University, Tallahassee
New College of Florida, Sarasota
University of Central Florida, Orlando
University of Florida, Gainesville
University of North Florida, Jacksonville
University of South Florida, Tampa
University of West Florida, Pensacola

# BACKPACKING
# FLORIDA

JOHNNY MOLLOY

University Press of Florida
Gainesville · Tallahassee · Tampa · Boca Raton
Pensacola · Orlando · Miami · Jacksonville · Ft. Myers · Sarasota

28  27  26  25  24  23    6  5  4  3  2  1

A record of the cataloguing-in-publication data is available from the Library of Congress.
ISBN 978-0-8130-8006-2 (pbk)

The University Press of Florida is the scholarly publishing agency for the State University System of Florida, comprising Florida A&M University, Florida Atlantic University, Florida Gulf Coast University, Florida International University, Florida State University, New College of Florida, University of Central Florida, University of Florida, University of North Florida, University of South Florida, and University of West Florida.

University Press of Florida
2046 NE Waldo Road
Suite 2100
Gainesville, FL 32609
http://upress.ufl.edu

# CONTENTS

SOUTH FLORIDA

# SIDEBARS

# INTRODUCTION

Looking for great places to go backpacking? The State of Florida is blessed with abundant tracts of wild lands, places where new and experienced backpackers can find attractive parcels laced with trails to trek, natural wonders to see, and sites to camp for days—or a day. These backpacking destinations present deep hardwood hammocks, open prairies, and remote pinelands—with alluring campsites to pitch your tent in the backcountry, where you can relax before a calming campfire and escape from the electronic chains that bind us to the daily grind.

A Florida backpacking adventure takes you places north and south, from the bluffs along Juniper Creek in the Panhandle to the glades of Big Cypress National Preserve, and a wealth of locales between. Florida's unforgettable backpacking jewels lead through federally designated wildernesses such as Bradwell Bay, deep in the Apalachicola National Forest, and coastal areas such as Moses Creek Conservation Area as well as along alluring waters such as the Saint Marys River at Ralph E. Simmons State Forest and beneath the big-sky prairies at Myakka River State Park.

Unbeknownst to most Americans, Florida is a backpacker's paradise, as evidenced by the Sunshine State's master path—the Florida Trail—running from the Big Cypress National Preserve to Gulf Islands National Seashore, more than 1,000 miles long and more in the making. It is the backbone of the backpacking trail network in Florida. The state's great national forests, parks, and preserves—the Apalachicola, Osceola, Ocala, Big Cypress, and Everglades—conserve millions of acres containing miles and miles of trails, presenting a multitude of overnighting opportunities that come as a true surprise to those who didn't know what fine backpacking opportunities await in Florida. Additionally, state parks, state forests, state water management districts, wildlife management areas, and other state lands offer numerous backpacking destinations within their boundaries.

So where to start backpacking in Florida? That is where this book comes into play. It delivers forty individual backpacking adventures covering more than 600 miles of trails, every mile of which I trekked and camped for this guide (whether I'd hiked them before or not, and nearly all of them I had). My résumé also includes having backpacked more than 2,500 nights in forty states throughout the United States, with hundreds of nights backpacked in Florida alone, including a complete thru-hike of the Florida Trail. That experience, combined with my having written more than eighty outdoor-related guidebooks on backpacking, hiking, camping, paddling, and bicycling, should give you confidence in this book, a guide to help you make the most of your time backpacking in Florida.

It all started with a backpacking trip at Great Smoky Mountains National Park back in my native Tennessee, an adventure that ultimately launched me into my career as an outdoor writer. As the backpacking trips continued, I learned to apply to life in general the lessons learned while in the back-country, such as persistence in the face of obstacles, patience when you have miles and miles to go, and acceptance of your circumstances when they are less than ideal. So can it be with you, whether you are new to backpacking or a rising veteran of the great outdoors.

To see regal woodlands, deep springs, and untamed wildlife—to back-pack Florida—and be able share them with you has brought me to the real-ization that purchasers of *Backpacking Florida* are banking their money and their free time that Johnny Molloy knows what he is talking about. This is serious business, and I take it seriously!

One of the greatest joys of my occupation is sharing my love of the out-doors with you. And as a man who has spent many a winter season ex-ploring Florida's natural lands and waters, my love of the state's ecological splendor raises the stakes even higher. I want y'all to see, smell, hear, and feel what lies out there, in the back of beyond, while backpacking Florida. As electronics further infiltrate every aspect of our lives, we are losing our connection with nature. Backpacking provides a means to get outside, to explore, to stimulate our mental, physical, and spiritual selves in the natural world.

You can hit the trail with friends and family, together discovering and sharing the God-given beauty of the Sunshine State. While backpacking Florida you can soak in horizon-to-horizon vistas in Kissimmee Prairie, wander among massive old-growth live oaks in Welaka State Forest, ramble alongside bucolic ponds in the Ocala National Forest, traipse through re-mote evergreen woodlands at Dupuis Wildlife Management Area (WMA), or visit the sinks and streams of Aucilla WMA.

This book includes different types of backpacks in varied settings with varying layers of difficulty. Most backpacking adventures detailed are two-night trips typical for the weekend backpacker, yet additional backpacks range from 3-mile, one-night family treks to multiday, 50-plus-mile, larger-than-life adventures.

The backpacks feature not only fine trails and campsites but also scenic sights—vast, open palmetto/wiregrass prairies broken by cypress domes; lush, wooded bottomlands along remote streams; boardwalks travers-ing otherwise inaccessible swamps; and fragrant pinelands pitted against a bright-blue sky. Well-known "must-do" destinations such as the Juniper Prairie Wilderness, Rice Creek Sanctuary, and the Blackwater River State Forest are included, but undiscovered gems like Jennings State Forest, Ocklawaha Prairie Restoration Area, and Bonnet Pond increase your Florida backpacking possibilities.

This book also delivers "must-know" information for you, so you can more adeptly execute successful backpacking adventures: how to get to the trailhead, how far the backpack is, the hike's difficulty, when to go, where the campsite are, what you are going to see along the way, and where you are, within reason, at any given moment of the hike. Each hike includes all of the above, along with an easy-to-scan map, trail mileage chart, and a photo to help you build a mental picture of the area. Additionally, scattered within this "where-to" guide are "how-to" backpacking tips and tricks guaranteed to make your outdoor adventures run more smoothly. These helpful tidbits will boost your quest for becoming the best backpacker you can be.

I hope this guide will inspire you to create your own adventures and make memories that will leave you and your loved ones wanting more, and to want to share the great outdoors with still others. The reason I travel and explore the outdoors is simple: the world is a beautiful place! Life is for living, and adventures are for having. Do everything now. Don't wait. Go now. Backpacking in Florida can be so exciting—you never know what is going to happen next, what is around the bend along the trail, what is over the next hill, or what the weather will bring. But I can guarantee you that using *Backpacking Florida* will bring a wealth of adventures and memories to last a lifetime.

## Backpacking in Florida

Look at a map of Florida. Several things will strike aspiring Sunshine State backpackers. First, the state extends from the western boundary with Alabama in the north across the Tallahassee Hills to the coastal estuaries of the Saint Marys River near Jacksonville, then down over the sandy hills of the central peninsula intermingled with rivers and wetlands aplenty to scattered prairies down to the sea of grass known as the Everglades. *Backpacking Florida* includes overnight trips traveling through all the far-flung points of the Sunshine State. These varied destinations harbor wide-ranging ecosystems containing diverse flora and fauna, augmenting your outdoor experience.

Furthermore, Florida is blessed with a wealth of public lands where you can enjoy backpacking—national parks, national forests, as well as state parks, forests, and water management districts. Big Cypress National Preserve offers America's most unique backpacking—bar none. Additional federal lands offer more backpacking possibilities—starting with Florida's national forests. Between the Apalachicola, Ocala, and Osceola National Forests, we have almost 1.2 million acres of trail-laced wildlands in which to overnight. Florida state parks preserve another 750,000-plus acres in which to backpack. Florida's state forests cover another million-plus acres where you can trek and pitch your tent. Finally, Florida's five water management districts, in the course of managing the state's aquatic reserve, also manage the trail-rich lands through which their waters flow, including still more backpacking opportunities. This adds up to a lot of Florida to explore by foot, enhancing the experience via overnight backpacking.

The diversity of terrain, habitat, and trails is reflected in the backpacking adventures that you can undertake here in Florida. Starting in the Panhandle, you can tackle a 28-mile adventure, complete with trail shelters, at Blackwater River State Forest; overnight on a coastal island at St. George Island State Park; tackle the surprisingly steep hills of Torreya State Park; or take a longer, wilder trek at vast Apalachicola National Forest, including the celebrated Bradwell Bay Wilderness.

North Florida has its own destinations, including the remote pinelands of the Osceola National Forest. The backcountry hike at Moses Creek ends on a bluff above an eye-catching tidal stream. Pitch your tent at a cool campsite on the shores of the St. Johns River at Bayard Conservation Area. Or take an extended ramble along the legendary Suwannee River.

Moving south, you come to Central Florida. Soak in distant panoramas while trekking through Bull Creek WMA. Take a pair of longer backpacks through the Ocala National Forest, home of the world's largest sand pine scrub ecosystem. Make a shorter trek through the varied landscapes at Ross Prairie State Forest. Wander through thick forests of the Withlacoochee River on the Richloam Tract. Ramble under a cathedral of live oaks and palms at Seminole State Forest or camp overnight in the back of beyond at Tosohatchee WMA. Explore part of the famed Green Swamp, headwaters of several Florida rivers. Loop your way through the wilds of Lake Wales Ridge State Forest.

South Florida offers immense wildlands ready to explore. First and foremost is Big Cypress National Preserve, where you tackle the first 30 miles of the Florida Trail through hiking terrain unlike anywhere else in North America. Both Myakka River State Park and Myakka State Forest present sizeable tracts with multiday overnight opportunities. Camp at beautiful and remote Bowman Island on the Ocean-to-Lake Trail. Head out to Kitching Creek at Jonathan Dickinson State Park.

When you ponder the possibilities, Florida is truly blessed with a wealth of backpacking opportunities.

## Weather

Given its warm climate, Florida definitely has a backpacking season. Starting in the north, from mid-October—when cool autumn fronts sweep over the Panhandle and North Florida—until April's end is generally the backpacking season up that way. The farther south you go, the shorter the backpacking season, but even in deep South Florida, backpackers can venture into the wild from mid-November through March, allowing for plenty of adventures under the stars. Generally speaking, December through March, with mild temperatures and less rainfall, present nearly idyllic backpacking conditions in the Sunshine State. Summer backpacking in Florida is untenable—too much heat and too many thunderstorms and mosquitoes. You will have a better experience when you are in the right place at the right time.

The following is a weather chart for Clermont, in Central Florida, giving a basic estimate for you to consider when to undertake your Sunshine State backpacking adventures.

| Month | Average high (degrees) | Average low (degrees) | Precipitation (inches) |
|---|---|---|---|
| January | 71 | 47 | 2.9 |
| February | 73 | 50 | 2.6 |
| March | 78 | 54 | 3.8 |
| April | 83 | 59 | 2.3 |
| May | 89 | 65 | 3.1 |
| June | 91 | 71 | 8.3 |
| July | 92 | 73 | 7.0 |
| August | 92 | 73 | 7.3 |
| September | 89 | 72 | 5.1 |
| October | 84 | 66 | 2.5 |
| November | 78 | 58 | 4.5 |
| December | 72 | 51 | 2.9 |

# HOW TO USE THIS GUIDEBOOK

This guidebook covers backpacking adventures throughout Florida. The backpacks are divided into four primary regions—Panhandle, North Florida, Central Florida, and South Florida. The following is a sample of what you find in the information box at the beginning of each Florida backpack:

# Bull Creek Backpack

## Overview

Superior scenery makes this loop backpack a winner. Known for its palmetto and wiregrass prairies with distant views, this circuit also leads you past cypress domes, sand pine scrub, and along Bull Creek using a historic railroad grade. Generally done as a long one-nighter, this trek can easily be stretched to two nights.

**Distance & Configuration**: 17.5-mile loop
**Difficulty**: Moderate, does have open, sunny stretches
**Outstanding Features**: Distant views, varied habitats, historic railroad grade
**Scenery**: 5
**Solitude**: 3
**Family-Friendly**: 2
**Canine-Friendly**: 3
**Fees/Permits**: None required
**Best Season**: Late October through March
**Maps**: Herky Huffman/Bull Creek Wildlife Management Area (WMA)
**For More Info**: Bull Creek WMA, FWC Northeast Region, Northeast Region, 1239 SW 10th St, Ocala, FL 34471-0323, 352-732-1225, https://myfwc.com/
**Finding the Trailhead**: From exit 180 on I-95 west of Melbourne, take US 192 west for 19.2 miles to turn left onto Crabgrass Road. Follow it for 6 miles as it heads southeasterly to enter Bull Creek WMA. The backpack starts at the campground entrance to the right, just before reaching the wildlife check station. GPS trailhead coordinates: 28.083101, -80.962788

The description begins with a short overview of the backpack, to give you a flavor of the adventure. It is followed by an information box. From the information box, we can see that the trip is a 17.5-mile loop trek, and its difficulty is labeled as moderate, mainly due to distance. Along the way you will enjoy views in the prairies as well as varied forests and also trek a historic railroad grade along the way.

Four rated hike descriptors follow—Scenery, Solitude, Family-Friendly, and Canine-Friendly. The descriptors are rated on a scale of 1 to 5, with 5 being the highest/best and 1 being the lowest/least. The "Scenery" on the above backpack is rated a 5 on a scale of 1 to 5, meaning the scenery is among the best in the state. Therefore, expect a scenic trip. "Solitude" is rated a 3, so you should expect company somewhere along the hike. The "Family-Friendly" score is a 2, meaning it can be challenging as a family backpacking destination, mainly because of open terrain. The "Canine-Friendly" rating is a 3 as the hike is relatively dry by Florida standards. The lower the number, the less friendly the backpack is for your dog. No fees or permits are required to undertake this hike, but any such requirements will be indicated at "Fees/Permits." "Best Season" lets you know the prime times to enjoy the backpack.

"Maps" tells you the best maps to use for the backpack. A high-quality map is included with each hike description in this guide and should suffice. However, bring the recommended map to augment the book map. "For More Info" tells you the governing body of the area backpacked, as well as pertinent phone numbers and websites for further research on your own and to obtain a camping permit. This is followed by "Finding the Trailhead," which provides trailhead directions along with trailhead coordinates you can plug into your device to get you there.

Following that is a rendition of the backpack, including campsite locations, water access points, and other must-know tips for the trek, as well as not-to-be-missed highlights and what to expect while out there—the feeling, the vibe of the adventure. Each hike description ends with "Mileages," a quick reference table of mileages and milestones along the way.

Some backpacks include an informational sidebar. The sidebars, usually accompanied with a lesson learned on the trail, offer tips and advice to help you become a better and more complete backpacker. Most sidebars are paired with particular backpacks because those backpacking trips likely have a scenario where the sidebar applies.

# BACKPACKER CHECKLIST

There is a reason why "hike your own hike" is a popular phrase in backpacking circles. Items needed for a backpacking trip that are dear to me may not seem essential to you. A way to determine what you (and your group) need is to go down this list, assemble the items, then get out there and hit the trail. After each trip, assess your gear. Did you bring everything you needed? Did you need everything you brought? Next, adjust your gear list for the next trip, continuing to refine your list.

In order to execute the best trip possible, go through the following sequence of questions and considerations:

First, contemplate these considerations:

Physical ability, trip desires, and expectations—What are the physical abilities of you and your party? What length and duration of trip do you desire? What are the group expectations? Are you each carrying your own food/gear or sharing gear? What is the weather forecast?

Now, go from your feet to your scalp to determine what clothing you will need. Next check the needs of your shelter, bedroom, bathroom, and kitchen. Other miscellaneous gear possibilities follow. The goal is to take everything you need and not one item more.

## Shoes

- Hiking shoes/boots
- Camp shoes/sandals

## Clothes

- Socks
- Long pants
- Short pants
- T-shirt
- Long-sleeve button-up shirt with collar
- Vest
- Jacket/poncho
- Bandanna
- Hat/toboggan

- Gloves
- Head net
- Extra clothes as needed or desired
- Backpack

## Shelter

- Tent, tarp, or under the stars
- Hammock

## Bedroom

- Closed-cell sleeping pad
- Ultralight air mattress
- Sleeping bag
- Pillow

## Bathroom

- Toothbrush/paste/floss
- Toilet paper
- Lotion
- Biodegradable soap
- Pack towel

## Kitchen

- Food, spices
- Water purification: filter, tablets, boil
- Cookware: cup, spoon, knife, pot, potholder, frying pan, spatula, tongs
- Cooking sources: Stove or fire/grill

## Other Stuff

- Trekking poles
- Ultralight camp chair
- Maps
- Compass
- Sunscreen

- Bug dope
- Lighter
- Fire starter
- Medical kit
- Cord—enough to hang food away from bears
- Headlamp, lantern, solar-powered light
- Other items to consider: Phone/cord/solar charger, spare batteries, trash bag, GPS, weather radio, aspirin, prescriptions, book, radio, camera, cards, vitamins, watch, lip balm, extra batteries, sunglasses, small towel, binoculars, wildlife identification books/apps

Just remember, backpacking Florida is about the experience, not the stuff you carry. Be prepared, but prepare to enjoy your time interacting with nature. My personal rule of thumb is to carry no more than 15 percent of my body weight, and closer to 10 percent if I can get away with it. Use this rule of thumb for yourself, no matter your weight. It will work for your kids, too.

Most importantly, carve out some free time to get out there and make some memories backpacking Florida.

# BACKPACK SUMMARY CHART

| Hike | Distance | Difficulty | Highlights |
|------|----------|-----------|------------|
| **PANHANDLE** | | | |
| 1 Blackwater Backpack | 28.7 | Difficult | Attractive waterways, elevation changes, trail shelters |
| 2 Torreya Backpack | 14.2 | Difficult | Distant vistas, clear streams, hills galore |
| 3 Fort Braden Backpack | 5.7 | Easy | Lakeside camping, great campsites, family backpack |
| 4 Bonnet Pond Backpack | 6.6 | Easy | Vast forest, good campsite |
| 5 St. George Island Backpack | 6.4 | Easy | Oceanic backpacking, great campsites |
| 6 Apalachicola Backpack | 32.5 | Difficult | Sopchoppy River, untamed wilderness |
| 7 Aucilla River Backpack | 14.4 | Moderate | Aucilla River, hardwood hammock forests |
| **NORTH FLORIDA** | | | |
| 8 Suwannee River Backpack | 50.9 | Difficult | River scenes, good campsites, long-distance opportunity |
| 9 Osceola Backpack | 16.3 | Moderate | Vast forests, trail shelter |
| 10 Saint Marys Backpack | 7.8 | Easy | Outstanding campsites, good trail conditions |
| 11 North Fork Backpack | 5.2 | Easy | Ecosystem variety, good reservable campsite |
| 12 Bayard Backpack | 7.1 | Easy | Riverside camp, well-marked and -maintained trails |
| 13 Moses Creek Backpack | 11.6 | Easy | Coastal hike, great campsite, views from campsite |
| 14 Rice Creek Sanctuary | 8.8 | Easy-moderate | Gorgeous swamp hardwood forest, Hoffman Crossing |
| **CENTRAL FLORIDA** | | | |
| 15 Welaka State Forest Backpack | 4.1 | Easy | Little Lake George, excellent campsites |
| 16 Holly Hammock Backpack | 3.1 | Easy | Varied ecosystems, good family backpack |
| 17 Ocklawaha Prairie Backpack | 5.0 | Easy | Wildlife observation tower, good campsite |
| 18 Ocala North Backpack | 39.1 | Difficult | Juniper Prairie Wilderness, Hopkins Prairie, Lake Ocklawaha |

| | | | |
|---|---|---|---|
| 19 Ocala South Backpack | 28.0 | Moderate-difficult | Farles Prairie, ponds, good campsites |
| 20 Saint Francis Backpack | 7.8 | Easy | Florida history, hammock woods |
| 21 Seminole State Forest Backpack | 11.4 | Moderate | Trail shelter, Black Water Creek, good campsites |
| 22 St. Johns River Backpack | 4.0 | Easy | Great campsites, family backpack |
| 23 Citrus Loop Backpack | 32.4 | Difficult | Big circuit, geology, good campsites |
| 24 Croom Tract Backpack | 11.3 | Moderate | Good campsites, hills |
| 25 Richloam Loop Backpack | 27.5 | Moderate-difficult | Swamp forests, big loop |
| 26 Green Swamp West Backpack | 15.0 | Easy-moderate | Varied terrain, good designated campsites |
| 27 Tosohatchee Backpack | 14.9 | Moderate | Palm/live oak hammocks, variety of ecosystems |
| 28 Bull Creek Backpack | 17.5 | Moderate | Distant views, varied habitats, historic railroad grade |
| 29 Three Lakes Backpack | 11.3 | Moderate | Hardwood hammocks, lake views, good campsites |
| 30 Lake Wales Ridge Backpack | 20.1 | Moderate-difficult | Scenery, reservable campsites, backwoods streams |
| 31 Kissimmee Prairie Backpack | 4.6 | Easy | Certified dark sky park, great campsite, big views |
| 32 Saint Sebastian Backpack | 5.4 | Easy | Quality, riverside campsite |

## SOUTH FLORIDA

| | | | |
|---|---|---|---|
| 33 Myakka River State Park Backpack | 29.2 | Difficult | Prairie views, varied environments, good campsites |
| 34 Myakka State Forest Backpack | 14.0 | Moderate | Great campsites, easy, well-marked trails |
| 35 Collier-Seminole Backpack | 7.5 | Difficult | Swamp hiking, mangrove woods |
| 36 Big Cypress Backpack | 31.5 | Difficult | Stunning scenery, challenge, remoteness |
| 37 Big Cypress North Loop Backpack | 15.3 | Moderate | First-rate scenery, good campsites, mostly dry footing |
| 38 Dupuis Loop Backpack | 15.4 | Moderate | Remoteness, scenery |
| 39 Bowman Island Backpack | 12.2 | Moderate-difficult | Hardwood hammock campsite, wetlands |
| 40 Jonathan Dickinson Backpack | 10.7 | Easy | Kitching Creek, flatwoods views |

# BEST FLORIDA BACKPACKING TRIPS BY CATEGORY

## Best Backpacks for Beginners

## Best Backpacks for Families

## Best Backpacks for Stream/River Lovers

## Best Backpacks for Pond/Lake Lovers

## Best Backpacks for Hill Seekers

## Best Backpacks for Views

## Best Swamp Backpacks

## Best Backpacks for Solitude

## Best Long Backpacks

# *Panhandle*

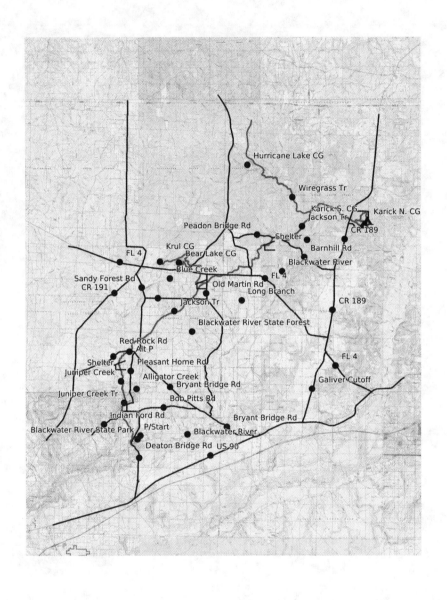

Hurricane Lake CG

Wiregrass Tr

Karick S. CG    Karick N. CG
Jackson Tr
CR 189

Peadon Bridge Rd
Shelter
Krul CG                Barnhill Rd
Bear Lake CG         Blackwater River
Blue Creek

Sandy Forest Rd              FL 4
CR 191
FL 4              Old Martin Rd
Jackson Tr        Long Branch        CR 189

Blackwater River State Forest

Red Rock Rd
Alt P
Shelter      Pleasant Home Rd
Juniper Creek                              FL 4
Alligator Creek
Bryant Bridge Rd       Galiver Cutoff
Juniper Creek Tr
Bob Pitts Rd
Indian Ford Rd
Blackwater River State Park    P/Start    Bryant Bridge Rd
Blackwater River
Deaton Bridge Rd   US 90

# 1

## Blackwater Backpack

### Overview

One of my personal favorites, this end-to-end backpack takes place in the Blackwater River State Forest, where red clay hills give way to sandy bottoms through which absolutely beautiful streams flow. First, tread over evergreen hills to then hike alongside gorgeous Juniper Creek, then roll the high ridge dividing Blackwater River from Juniper Creek before crossing the Blackwater River and making your way to trail's end at Karick Lake. Three trail shelters are scattered along with the route, enhancing the camping possibilities.

---

**Distance & Configuration**: 28.7-miles end-to-end
**Difficulty**: Difficult due to distance
**Outstanding Features**: Attractive waterways, elevation changes, trail shelters
**Scenery**: 4
**Solitude**: 4
**Family-Friendly**: 1
**Canine-Friendly**: 3
**Fees/Permits**: Parking permits required
**Best season**: November through April
**Maps**: Blackwater River State Forest Map
**For More Info**: Blackwater River State Forest, 11650 Munson Hwy, Milton, FL 32570, 850-957-5700, https://www.fdacs.gov/
**Finding the Trailhead**: To reach the hike's northern terminus from the intersection of US 90 and FL 4 west of Crestview, take FL 4 west for 4.6 miles. Then turn right onto FL 189 north, and follow it for 7.7 miles to turn right onto Upper Karick Lake Road. Follow it for 0.9 miles, then turn right and follow the road into Karick Lake *North* Campground. To reach the hike's beginning, backtrack to FL 189 and take it south for 8.6 miles to turn right onto Galiver Cutoff. Follow it for 4.5 miles and then turn right onto US 90 west. Follow it for 8.3 miles and then turn right onto Deaton Bridge Road. Follow it 4.5 miles to the Blackwater River State Park entrance on your right. Enter the state park

and pay your overnight parking fee and park where directed. GPS trailhead coordinates: Karick Lake North—30.896432, -86.641741; Blackwater River State Park—30.709661, -86.876656

---

Florida's largest state forest, coming in at 213,508 acres, the Blackwater presents plenty of room to roam and some fine trails upon which to backpack. Set in the western end of the Panhandle fast against the Alabama state line, this alluring preserve is laced with numerous swift-water streams coursing through hilly terrain that is further improved with hiking trails. The state forest offers recreationalists a wonderment of options—river and lake paddling, fishing, hunting, campground camping, and, of course, backpacking. By combining the Juniper Creek Trail and the Jackson Trail, backpackers can undertake a fine tour of the forest along the way, with elevation changes of ±1,400 feet over the course of the backpack. Your trip can be undertaken in two to three nights, depending on your whims. Water is generally available but not immediately at two of the three trail shelters. Safe, fee parking is available at either end of the backpack.

Heading south to north, leave the overnight parking at Blackwater River State Park, walking the road back to the state park entrance. Cross Deaton Bridge Road and keep west to meet the Juniper Creek Trail at 0.4 mile. Here, head right and quickly bridge Green Branch, flowing dark in swamp woods. The single-track path heads north, crossing Green Branch a second time. Typically, the main stream is bordered by high-water stream braids also coursing through dense swamp woods. Rise into pine palmetto woods. You will cross occasional fire roads that sometimes serve as barriers for the frequent prescribed burns undertaken here in Blackwater.

Stay with the blazes as you work near private property; then, at 2.1 miles, cross paved Indian Ford Road. Reenter thickety, brushy woods with a hill rising to your right and unseen Juniper Creek to your left. At 3.0 miles, bridge swift, sand-bottomed Alligator Creek, another blackwater stream flowing through wide swamp woods. Rise into pines and oaks, crossing lesser tributaries of Juniper Creek, where Atlantic white cedars and cane form dense ranks.

By 3.7 miles, Juniper Creek comes into view. Note the sandbars on the stream bends. Stay in thick woods. Watch out for cypress knees on the trail and loblolly pines rising from the moist bottoms. Sparkleberry and titi close in. At 4.4 miles, turn back from the creek, passing overflow swamps. Rise along a hill, returning to Juniper Creek at 5.1 miles. At 5.7 miles, on a bluff above the creek, a spur goes right to the first trail shelter, a three-sided wooden affair with an open front and sleeping room for four. A fire ring and

Hike past this bluff above Juniper Creek.

benches are nearby. Water can be had from Juniper Creek. Ample tent sites are nearby.

Beyond the shelter, the stream and trail briefly separate. Resume along the waterway before climbing away at 6.5 miles to the signature clay bluffs for which this area is known. The red clay bluffs are steep and can be unstable. Keep back and help preserve them. Ahead, pass a spur trail right to a parking area before reaching and crossing Red Rock Road at 7.0 miles. Here, you join the Jackson Trail, also referred to as the Jackson Red Ground Trail. It climbs up to a longleaf wiregrass ecosystem. Here the Blackwater River State Forest and the adjoining Conecuh National Forest in Alabama form the world's largest remaining longleaf wiregrass habitation.

You will be in this ecosystem much of the trek from here on out. At 8.3 miles, cross paved Sandy Landing Road. Stay in high, dry woods, tracing the path off and on old forest roads, soaring to more than 200 feet in elevation. At 10.4 miles, dip to thicker woods as you skirt the upper drainage of Alligator Creek. Roll through hills before dropping to cross the headwaters of Blue Creek at 12.0 and 12.3 miles. At 12.5 miles, join Charley Foster Road to bridge upper Blue Creek; then climb a big hill before splitting left into pines.

At 13.1 miles, cross another tributary of Blue Creek on a wide boardwalk. Get water here if you are staying at the trail shelter ahead. At 13.6 miles,

Trekking past Karick Lake near the backpack's end.

reach the next trail shelter. This one faces north and is smaller (comfortably sleeping two) and less used, but it does have a picnic table. At 14.0 miles, just before crossing Old Martin Road, a spur goes left 2.4 miles to Bear Lake Recreation Area. (Old Martin Road is a potential water cache if staying at the nearby shelter.) We cross Old Martin Road in thick, oak-heavy woods, emerging on FL 4 at 15.3 miles to use the highway bridge to cross Beaver Creek.

At 15.6 miles, split left on McVay Road, then quickly veer right, back into woods on a hiker trail. At 16.1 miles, bridge not-muddy Muddy Branch, briefly tracing a logging tram before climbing into evergreens blanketing a hill, only to dip to span Long Branch at 16.9 miles. Come near a private property inholding, then cross paved Beaver Creek Road at 17.3 miles. After the crossing, the Jackson Trail abruptly turns north and spans a swift tributary of Blackwater River at 17.9 miles. Roll through youngish pines and turkey oak hills.

At 19.4 miles, take a boardwalk over a clear stream, coming to the final trail shelter at 19.8 miles, set in an attractive grove of live oaks. The small shelter is complemented with fire ring and picnic tables. Water can be had at the last stream crossed or a stream ahead on the trail. The Jackson Trail keeps north, emerging on Peadon Bridge Road at 20.4 miles. Head right on this road, bridging the beautiful Blackwater River at 20.9 miles. Continue east, splitting left from the road at 21.2 miles, back on foot trail in the woods.

Rise to high pines on the ridge dividing Blackwater River from its tributary Panther Creek. Cross occasional spring seeps. Look for pitcher plants in these wet areas. At 23.8 miles, come to a trail intersection and picnic table. Here, the Wiregrass Trail splits left, with 5 miles to Hurricane Lake and 7 miles from there to the Alabama state line. We stay with the Jackson Trail as it curves easterly, circling around steephead branches of Panther Creek, bridging Panther Creek on a forest road at 24.9 miles. Aim southeast, crossing sand forest roads and passing through smaller pines before popping out onto CR 189 at 26.9 miles.

From CR 189, keep east, reaching another trail intersection and picnic table at 27.3 miles. Here, the Karick Lake Loop goes left 2.1 miles to Karick Lake North Campground, but we stay straight with the Jackson Trail, coming to the access road for Karick Lake South Campground at 28.0 miles. Stay with the blazes as they lead to the shore of Karick Lake, where fine lake views await. Join the berm of the lake dam, crossing it to circle around a cove. Enter Karick Lake North Campground and finish the backpack at 28.7 miles, completing the Panhandle backpacking adventure.

## Mileages

| | |
|---|---|
| 0.0 | Blackwater River State Park overnight parking |
| 0.4 | Right on Juniper Creek Trail |
| 3.0 | Bridge Alligator Creek |
| 5.7 | Trail shelter |
| 7.0 | Cross Red Rock Road |
| 8.3 | Cross Sandy Landing Road |
| 12.5 | Bridge Blue Creek on Charley Foster Road |
| 13.6 | Trail shelter |
| 15.3 | Bridge Beaver Creek on FL 4 |
| 19.8 | Trail shelter |
| 20.9 | Bridge Blackwater River on Peadon Bridge Road |
| 23.8 | Wiregrass Trail heads left; stay on Jackson Trail |
| 26.9 | Cross CR 189 |
| 28.0 | Karick Lake South Campground |
| 28.7 | Karick Lake North Campground trailhead |

## Choose the Right Backpack for Your Hike

Backpacks have come a long way in the past fifty years. I'm talking about backpacks used for overnight excursions as opposed to daypacks used for school, work, and day hiking. In the bad old days, backpacks were a simple aluminum frame holding a nylon pack with a few pockets. Unpadded straps went over your shoulders and around your waist. Known as external packs (due to the external aluminum frame), these became more deluxe, with padded shoulder straps, waist belt, and a dizzying array of pockets for stowing your gear.

External packs served well in their day. My longest non-resupplied back-pack ever—fifteen nights in Great Smoky Mountains National Park—was done with an external pack. As time rolled on, the internal backpack came into vogue. As its name implies, the frame is built into the pack.

Today, internal frame packs have supplanted external frame packs in popularity. Sure, there are still a few external frame backpacks out there, but internal frames rule the roost. I use only internal packs these days.

Internal packs fit closer to your body and are more compact, whereas external frame packs are generally bigger and bulkier but have more pockets, which help in organization and loading. Internal pack users have to take more of a "duffel bag" approach to their loading, though assorted pockets and pouches are incorporated into most internal packs. Most importantly, internal packs are significantly lighter. The lightest is a mere 1.5 pounds, though they are more often around 3 pounds, versus 5 pounds for your average external pack.

For the backpacker, which pack you choose is a matter of personal taste. For example, when going off trail or on shorter trips, I prefer a sturdy—albeit heavier—internal pack. Internal packs are narrower and can squeeze through brush and between trees without catching. The sturdier internals are more durable.

The ultralight internal packs are designed for longer treks, typically Appalachian Trail thru-hikers going ultralight head-to-toe. The ultralight internals are designed to be carried on cleared, maintained trails and are less sturdy or durable. Consider a more durable internal pack when backpacking through Florida's Apalachicola National Forest, where less-maintained trails can be rough on a pack.

Your starting point for choosing a backpack is fit. Head to your nearest outdoor store and try on various packs, or borrow a friend's pack. Switch packs with someone while on a trip. The more types of packs you try, the more likely you are to find one suiting your needs. Specialty outdoor retailers often rent packs.

Ask yourself the following questions: How much money do you want to spend? How often do you plan to backpack? How long is your typical trip? Name-brand packs offer quality and durability. Consider how much gear you like to carry. Do you like to bring everything but the kitchen sink? Or do you carry only the barest of necessities?

If you want to pare down your gear, buy a smaller pack. Far too often, I see backpackers with huge packs designed for a two-week trip when their average trip is two days. And if you go on a longer trip, cinch gear and extra supplies to your smaller pack. No matter how long you go, be discerning when choosing the right pack for your backpacking adventures.

# 2

## Torreya Backpack

### Overview

Mile for mile, this is the hilliest backpack in Florida. Set in bluffs and bottoms along the Apalachicola River at Torreya State Park, make a figure-eight loop that includes river views, wildflowers, Civil War history, and three reservable backcountry campsites to pitch your tent along the way.

---

**Distance & Configuration**: 14.2-mile figure-eight loop

**Difficulty**: Difficult due to elevation change

**Outstanding Features**: Distant vistas, clear streams, hills galore

**Scenery**: 5

**Solitude**: 3

**Family-Friendly**: 3

**Canine-Friendly**: 3

**Fees/Permits**: Camping fee plus entrance fee required

**Best Season**: Late October through mid-April

**Maps**: Torreya State Park

**For More Info**: Torreya State Park, 2576 NW Torreya Park Rd, Bristol, FL 32321, 850-643-2674, https://www.floridastateparks.org/

**Finding the Trailhead**: From downtown Bristol, take FL 12 east for 6.5 miles. Turn left on Torreya Park Road and follow it for 7 miles to enter the state park. Stay with the main park road to reach the Gregory House. GPS trailhead coordinates: 30.576315, -84.948702

---

Even after you've been warned of the hills at Torreya State Park, this backpack will surprise. The entire adventure presents a whopping 2,250 feet of ups and 2,250 feet of downs along its course. In un-Florida-like fashion, the trails here swoop down from bluffs and hills to sandy, clear, swift-bottomed creeks only to rise again—and then repeat the same process over and over. The state park forest is still recovering from Hurricane Michael back in 2018, leaving the paths more open and brushy, but don't let that deter you. The

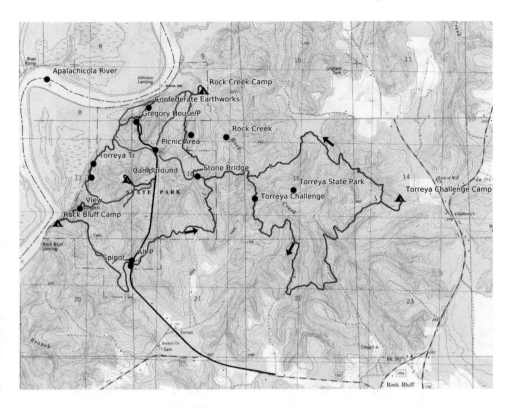

three backcountry campsites are all reservable (by phone, call the park office) and offer fine places to overnight. Each camp has multiple sites offering fire rings, benches, and tenting spots. Stream water is near each site. Additionally, the park has portable restrooms near the camps.

Since the backpack is comprised of two individual loops linked by a connector trail, you can do a shorter one-night circuit using only the Torreya Trail or double your pleasure making a two-night trip incorporating the aptly named Torreya Challenge. Either way, a backpack here will leave your legs and lungs humming. Backpackers planning trips in the Appalachian Mountains use Torreya as a training ground.

The park is named for the rare torreya tree. Only some two hundred survive in the wild. The evergreen grows only in Liberty and Gadsden Counties in Florida, with a stronghold in this park. Start your adventure at the Gregory House, built in 1849 and moved to its present location in the 1930s. The commanding heights rise 150 feet above the Apalachicola River.

Start your backpack from the rear of the Gregory House. Looking out on the river, head left on a blue-blazed trail. All connector trails (no names) are blazed in blue, whereas the Torreya Trail and the Torreya Challenge Trail

Phlox graces the trailside on this wildflower-rich backpack.

are blazed in orange. Descend west on a sharp slope cloaked in magnolia, sweetgum, and pines. At 0.3 mile, cross the first of numerous sandy, clear, spring seeps, then head left, joining the single-track Torreya Trail. Immediately climb past a spur leading left to the park picnic area.

At 0.7 mile, come near the river slough. Up and down we go. Note the trillium, violets, and toothwort among other wildflowers that rise in spring. At 1.3 miles, another spur heads left to the auto-accessible campground, but we stay right with the Torreya Trail, bridging a clear spring seep. Climb 215-foot Logan Hill and enjoy a view of the river and lands west at 1.5 miles. At 1.8 miles, split right toward popular Rock Bluff Camp, set on a rolling ridge and sporting a river view of its own.

The Torreya Trail turns east from the Apalachicola River, climbing all the while on a double-track, passing a spur left to the park entrance trailhead at 2.5 miles. Continue the uptick, skirting unusual red-rock bluffs among scattered evergreens. Cross the park entrance road at 3.3 miles. Note the convenient roadside water spigot. The path now descends into the steep headwaters of Rock Creek, into a chasm of sorts, bridging clear creeks and then climbing per the pattern of Torreya State Park. Back down we go, tackling lesser streams and hills. Look for beech trees among the north-facing hills.

Reach an intersection at 4.8 miles. Here, we head right, leaving the Torreya Trail on a blue-blazed connector toward aptly named Torreya Challenge. The trail is less worn here. Work easterly, nearing Rock Creek before reaching the loop portion of the hike at 5.3 miles. Begin the clockwise continuously hilly trek, southbound up and over hills and then down into fern-lined spring seeps, many of them bridged. You'll go on and off a few old jeep roads, but the trail remains mostly single-track.

Bridge upper Rock Creek at 8.2 miles. The ensuing climb shows why would-be mountain backpackers train here at Torreya State Park. At 8.9 miles, the spur to Torreya Challenge Camp splits right, past a clear area, then left down into woods where several camps are set on a hill above a noisy stream. Backtrack to the Torreya Challenge, continuing the pronounced undulations. Descend from a high point at 10.8 miles, bridging Rock Creek before completing the Torreya Challenge circuit at 11.6 miles. From here, backtrack on the connector, resuming the Torreya Trail at 12.1 miles. Keep west, crossing a tributary on the Stone Bridge and splitting right at 12.2 miles. Naturally, a climb is in order. Then you descend to trek along a tributary of Rock Creek, making an intersection here at 13.2 miles. Split right for Rock Creek Camp, a series of sites on a hill above the stream. I recommend site 3.

Backtrack, and then come near the river again after passing a trail to the picnic area. At 13.9 miles, take the blue-blazed connector toward the Gregory House, passing the locale where Confederate soldiers were entrenched above the Apalachicola River, 95 miles from the Gulf, dissuading the Union from using the waterway to move troops and supplies. Rest on this final uphill while you read the interpretive information. At 14.2 miles, return to the Gregory House, having climbed 2,250 feet and descended 2,250 feet—in Florida!

## Mileages

0.0  Gregory House
1.5  View from Logan Hill
1.8  Rock Bluff Camp
3.3  Cross park entrance road, spigot
5.3  Begin Torreya Challenge
8.9  Spur to Torreya Challenge Camp
11.6  Finish Torreya Challenge
13.2  Spur to Rock Creek Camp
14.2  Gregory House

# 3

## Fort Braden Backpack

### Overview

Tackle surprisingly steep terrain amid a slope and ravine hardwood forest of beech, tulip, and other trees as you combine two loops in the Fort Braden Tract of Lake Talquin State Forest. Two reservable camps overlooking striking Lake Talquin await. The scenery, including crystal-clear sandy streams, pleases the eye not only at the camp but throughout the excellent one-night backpack.

**Distance & Configuration**: 5.7-mile loop

**Difficulty**: Easy, does have hills

**Outstanding Features**: Lakeside camping, great campsites, family backpack

**Scenery**: 5

**Solitude**: 2

**Family-Friendly**: 5

**Canine-Friendly**: 4

**Fees/Permits**: Parking fee, campsite fee

**Best Season**: October through April

**Maps**: Fort Braden Tract Lake Talquin State Forest

**For More Info**: Lake Talquin State Forest, 865 Geddie Rd, Tallahassee, FL 32304, 850-681-5953, https://www.fdacs.gov/; https://www.reserveamerica.com/

**Finding the Trailhead**: From the intersection of Capitol Circle NW and FL 20, west of downtown Tallahassee, take FL 20 west for 8.7 miles. Look for a sign stating "Lake Talquin Fort Braden Trails." Turn right off SR 20 and travel just a short distance to reach the trailhead. GPS trailhead coordinates: 30.439739, -84.495435

This backpack takes place on the steep slopes and shoreline of beautiful Lake Talquin, part of Lake Talquin State Forest, specifically the Fort Braden Tract, where three interconnected hiker-only loops add up to 9-plus miles of pathways—and two fine backcountry campsites for backpackers like us. A set of horse trails (not shown on accompanying map) also winds through

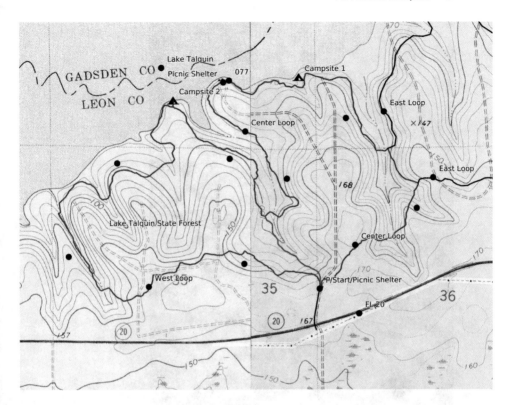

the area, occasionally using the same track as the hiker trails, but this doesn't pose a problem as the paths are separately signed and blazed. Just keep an eye peeled for the orange hiker blazes and you will be fine.

The large trailhead features an information kiosk, restroom, and picnic shelter. Pay your modest parking fee and make sure you have reserved your chosen campsite through https://www.reserveamerica.com/. Start on the hiker-only, orange-blazed trails. Enter the woods at a sign stating "Center Loop to West Loop Trails." Walk just a few feet and then split left with the West Loop on the upper end of a slope. Magnolia, pine, holly, and sweetbay trees collude to keep the forest green year-round, complemented by beech and sweetgum trees aplenty. At 0.1 mile, cross via boardwalk the first of several spring branches emanating from the hillside along which the trail travels before returning to the hilltop. The higher ground harbors scrub oaks and pines, a drier and sandier environment. Watch as occasional fire roads and horse trails cross the hiker-only paths.

At 0.9 mile, the West Loop turns north for Lake Talquin. Hike along a spring branch emanating from a hill—known as a steephead around these parts—as it begins cutting a sharp yet closely wooded ravine, thick with

Spend the night at this campsite overlooking Lake Talquin.

ferns and beard cane. Level off as Lake Talquin come into view at 1.4 miles, where moss-draped cypress, pine, tulip trees, and sweetgum rise resplendent. Wind among squishy bottomland cut with clear, sandy, shallow watercourses and wooded drier hills. At 2.3 miles, a short trail goes left to Hike In Campsite 2. Here you will find a fine shoreline flat, shaded by beech, hickory, and magnolias, with partial lake views. A fire ring, tent sites, and picnic table complement the scene. The only downside—the camp is susceptible to a cold north wind.

The West Loop turns away from the lake, making a wide circle around another steephead branch after leaving the campsite. At 3.0 miles, come to an intersection. Here, split left, joining the Center Loop, turning north back toward beautiful Lake Talquin, one of Florida's prettiest impoundments. Traverse hilly terrain, crossing clear, sand-bottomed creeks. Return to the shoreline at 3.8 miles and then pop out onto a clearing, complemented with benches, a large fire ring, and picnic shelter. Don't be tempted to camp here, as the locale is for day use only. Instead, continue the Center Loop, savoring some shoreline hiking.

At 4.2 miles, come to Hike In Campsite 1. It is set on a peninsula beside a small lake cove. Slightly sloped, the camp has fine lake views and is bigger. At 4.5 miles, begin the climb from Lake Talquin, along another sandy crystalline stream. At 4.8 miles, in hilly terrain, pass the first of two intersections with the East Loop. Beyond the second intersection you will cut across some steep ravines rising to level woods, reaching the trailhead at 5.6 miles, completing the pretty, undulating overnighter.

## Mileages

0.0   Fort Braden trailhead
1.4   Come along Lake Talquin
2.3   Hike In Campsite 2
3.0   Join Center Loop
4.2   Hike In Campsite 1
5.6   Fort Braden trailhead

### About Water in the Backcountry

I drink untreated water. No, I'm not talking about down Mexico way (I did that and got sick). I'm talking about drinking water in the backcountry in the United States—and all over Florida, from the Panhandle to the Everglades. I've drunk from swamps in Louisiana and wilderness rivers in New Mexico. I've drunk from alpine lakes high in the California Sierras and iron-rich lakes in Minnesota, ponds in Maine, as well as from springs, creeks, and rivers in my home state of Tennessee.

Face it, while backpacking, we cannot bring all the water we will need to drink. That means we will have to obtain water from local sources. In the back of beyond, backpackers are faced with a dilemma: do I drink the water?

I am in the minority, but I drink the water directly from the source and don't treat it. To the chagrin of my backpacking compadres, I haven't gotten sick. However, consider the following do-as-I-say-not-as-I-do advice: treat your water.

Two of us were backpack fishing near Yellowstone's Heart Lake for several days. We drank the water directly from the area streams and lakes.

My fishing partner got sick from the water, and I didn't. The same thing happened while backpacking Michigan's Ottawa National Forest and Montana's Glacier National Park. (All of the above backpackers filter their water now.)

So what can drinking bad water do? Microbes such as giardia and cryptosporidium get in your intestines and disrupt your life with excessive gas, diarrhea, and other unpleasantries. Giardiasis—the illness caused by giardia—won't ruin your average backpacking trip, as it takes one to two weeks for symptoms to appear. But once the symptoms crop up, expect to be ill for two to six weeks. Weight loss and dehydration follow. A doctor's gut-relieving prescription and plenty of fluids may help with the symptoms, which will eventually run their course, resulting in one painful weight-loss program.

Treating your water has become a lot easier these days, but let's harken back for a moment. The old method was to boil your water for at least a minute—there's nothing like hot water to sate a big thirst! It is not convenient, either: you have to wait until after your water is boiled, which means you have to have made a fire or broken out a camp stove.

Then came the pump filters—you literally pump your water through a device that filters out the demon microorganisms. Pump filters were once bulky but are now smaller and commonly used. Many people use chemical water treatments.

Iodine was the choice of days gone by, but it has an awful taste and gives you iodine breath, which ain't good. Nowadays we have products like Aqua Mira, where you mix two drops of chemicals, making chlorine dioxide, and wait thirty minutes; then your water is fine. Again, the wait is a problem, but it is the lightest option. Buying a water bottle with a built-in filter is an easier choice. Simply fill your water bottle and then suck through a straw, which forces the water through a built-in small filter, which needs to be replaced often.

UV filters are another option—using ultraviolet rays to kill the bad things in the aqua. The flaw—these products, such as Steripen, use batteries, which can die.

Simple filters such as the gravity-fed Sawyer are lightweight, cheap, and last for years. They use special microbe-blocking membranes and operate using gravity—or squeeze pressure if you're in a hurry. Sawyer filters are used in developing countries throughout the world.

No matter your method, treating your water is smart. Otherwise, you may spend your time being sick instead of backpacking.

# 4

## Bonnet Pond Backpack

### Overview

This one-night trip on the Florida Trail takes you to a designated campsite in the vast Apalachicola National Forest. Leave developed Camel Lake Campground and wander southeast over low hills and along small streams to come to a fine overnighting spot under turkey oaks and pines, with lovely Bonnet Pond just a stone's throw away.

---

**Distance & Configuration**: 6.6-mile out-and-back
**Difficulty**: Easy
**Outstanding Features**: Vast forest, good campsite
**Scenery**: 4
**Solitude**: 3
**Family-Friendly**: 4
**Canine-Friendly**: 4
**Fees/Permits**: Parking fee
**Best Season**: October through April
**Maps**: Apalachicola National Forest
**For More Info**: Apalachicola National Forest, Apalachicola Ranger District Office, 11152 NW FL 20, Bristol, FL 32321, 850-643-2282; https://www.fs.usda.gov/
**Finding the Trailhead**: From the intersection of FL 20 and CR 12 in Bristol, take CR 12 south for 11.4 miles. Turn left onto FR 105 and follow it for 2.0 miles. Turn right into Camel Lake Recreation Area; then turn right again into the day-use area. Make sure to pay the day-use fee, even though you are parking overnight. GPS trailhead coordinates: 30.277055, -84.987247

---

Camel Lake is the starting point for this backpack that threads into one of the more remote locales in Florida, the Apalachicola National Forest. Though threaded with forest roads, the 574,000-acre wildland offers solitude for those who seek it. Established in 1936, the tract near Tallahassee holds

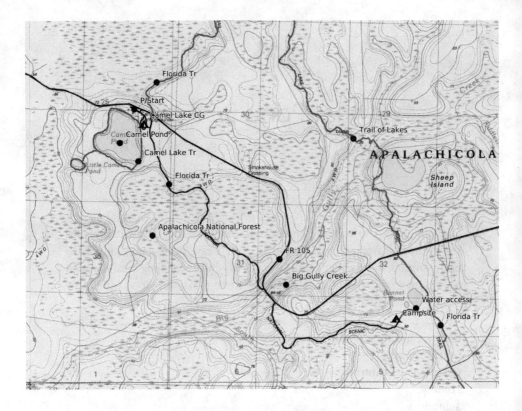

some of the more challenging stretches of the Florida Trail. This particular hike traverses an easier segment of the Florida Trail, starting at Camel Lake Recreation Area, with a fine campground, picnicking, and swimming area, including a trail encircling Camel Pond. (Yes, despite the recreation area being named Camel Lake, the body of water where the recreation area is situated is officially named Camel Pond.)

Name aside, this makes for an ideal starting point, safe parking, and a place to camp before or after your backpack if you so choose. Begin your backpacking adventure to Bonnet Pond by walking back out to Forest Road (FR) 105 and heading east, away from the way you drove in. After a few hundred feet, meet the Florida Trail as it crosses FR 105. Head right, south-bound, passing the Camel Lake camping area on your right. Continue south in pines, turkey oaks, and scattered clumps of saw palmetto. Ahead, you will cross numerous minor forest roads. Stay with the well-marked and -blazed Florida Trail.

At 0.5 mile, descend to work along a wooded wetland to your right, where Atlantic white cedars rise above titi thickets. At 0.6 mile, bridge a little streamlet ensconced in thick vegetation and then rise back to pines and

A chilly winter sun sets on the author near Bonnet Pond.

turkey oaks. The single-track path runs parallel to a thicket on your right. At 1.0 miles, dip into another titi thicket and then cross another small stream on a boardwalk. Climb out again into rolling hills.

At 1.9 miles, pop out on FR 105. Use the forest road span to cross over Big Gully Creek. At 2.0 miles split right off the forest road, returning to woods. Here, you traverse a slope rising from South Creek, walking the margin between streamside thickets and more open pine/oak complex. At 2.3 miles, circle around a revegetated sand pit and keep east along hills dropping off to wetlands.

At 3.3 miles, intersect the spur left to Bonnet Pond Camp. Here a fire ring, benches, and tent sites are located in a turkey oak and pine flat. The recommended site is just a short distance from Bonnet Pond. To reach Bonnet Pond and water, continue the Florida Trail beyond the campsite, then split left on a blue-blazed spur about 120 yards distant.

After enjoying a night under the stars, you can backtrack to Camel Lake Campground or continue a short distance on the Florida Trail to meet the Trail of Lakes. This less-used and less-maintained path splits left from the Florida Trail and works past Sheep Island Pond, crossing several streams. It can be quite a wet-footed walk as it reconnects with the Florida Trail north of Camel Lake and then joins the Florida Trail southbound to return to Camel Lake, making for a 9.5-mile circuit.

## Mileages

0.0   Camel Lake trailhead
1.9   Bridge Big Gully Creek on FR 105
3.3   Bonnet Pond Campsite
6.6   Camel Lake trailhead

# 5

## St. George Island Backpack

### Overview

Overnight on a Gulf of Mexico barrier island at St. George Island State Park. Start by trekking a boardwalk over dunes then along a wildlife-rich tidal estuary to reach a piney peninsula. Trek along old vegetated dunes to reach two open campsites presenting Apalachicola Bay.

**Distance & Configuration**: 6.4-mile out-and-back
**Difficulty**: Easy
**Outstanding Features**: Oceanic backpacking, great campsites
**Scenery**: 5
**Solitude**: 2
**Family-Friendly**: 4
**Canine-Friendly**: 3
**Fees/Permits**: Campsite fee
**Best Season**: October through April
**Maps**: St. George Island State Park
**For More Info**: St. George Island State Park, 1900 E Gulf Beach Dr, St. George Island, FL 32328, 850-927-2111; https://www.floridastateparks.org/
**Finding the Trailhead**: From the intersection of US 98 and FL 300/Island Drive in Eastpoint, head south on FL 300 for 5.6 miles to St. George Island. Turn left onto East Gulf Beach Drive and follow it 4.4 miles to enter St. George Island State Park and get your camping permit. Continue on the main park road for 2.2 miles to park at the East Slough Beach Access on your right. The East Slough Overlook Trail starts on the far side of the road from the parking area. GPS trailhead coordinates: 29.704476, -84.76240

Have you ever wanted to backpack and camp on the ocean? Well, here's your chance. St. George is one of the largest barrier islands on Florida's Gulf coast. The most easterly 2,000 acres are protected as a state park where

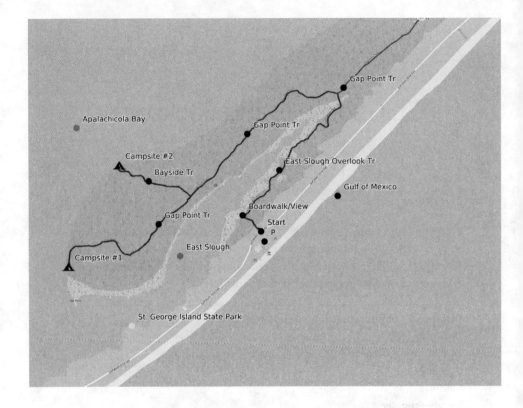

beaches, sand dunes, and pine trees overlook Apalachicola Bay, lying between St. George Island and the mainland.

Famed for its blinding-white beach sands rising from emerald ocean waters, the island's interior is scenic, too. Here sea oats grab a foothold, dunes begin, giving way to slash pine forest. Ponds and grasses dot the island interior, breaking up the woods where the turpentining industry came to milk the island's pines early in the twentieth century. While hiking to the campsites you can still see evidence of turpentining on many park pine trees along the interior island trail. Black, vertical barkless areas with "V"-shaped scars show where incisions were made in the tree by a galvanized metal gutter in winter. Next, a container was put below the gutter. Then, in summer, resin would flow into the container, known as a "gerty cup," a special kind of clay pot. This pine resin would be distilled into oil of turpentine, used for explosives, detergents, and in shipbuilding.

Start this oceanic backpack by joining the East Slough Overlook Trail as it leaves west from the main park road. An elevated boardwalk leads you over sensitive sand dunes and then gives way to wind-pruned scrub woods, with plenty of yaupon holly. Keep west, taking a spur to the East Slough

St. George Island offers you a chance to go on an oceanside backpack.

Overlook at 0.2 mile, a viewing deck overlooking tidal East Slough. Your camping destinations are located among the pines on the far side of East Slough.

Next, turn northeast, with East Slough to your left and black needlerush bordering the tidal waters. At 0.5 mile, cross three bridges in succession over wetlands. At 0.8 mile, bridge the main feeder stream leading into East Slough, then reach a trail intersection in a large, piney flat. Here, at 0.9 mile, head left on the Gap Point Trail. (To the right, the Gap Point Trail leads to the park campground, an alternate starting point.) Head southwest into the main peninsula, winding past many old, tapped pines. A few live oaks find their places.

At 1.8 miles, look across East Slough back to where you were. At 2.0 miles, reach an intersection. Here, the Bayside Trail splits right. For now, keep straight, heading toward Gap Point. Views open as you near the shore. Come along the melding of land and water and then turn south, reaching Campsite 1, actually two sites, set along the water in a smattering of pines, bordered in low brush, at 2.8 miles. Each of the two sites here offers a picnic table and fire ring. Depending upon the moment, tidal flats or shallow waters extend from the shore, and distant vistas stretch to the horizon. At night, the lights of the mainland twinkle in the distance. Now this is Florida backpacking!

From Campsite 1, backtrack to the Bayside Trail and then turn left, weaving around low wet areas to emerge at Campsite 2 at 4.0 miles. This campsite looks north and features a small beach of sorts, with extensive tidal shallows, a generally sandier area. Beware: shade is limited. But the views are worth it. By the way, you must carry all your own freshwater to the backcountry campsites here at St. George Island. Also, call the office ahead of time to make reservations for these backcountry camps during predictably busy times. Leaving Campsite 2, it is a simple backtrack to the East Slough beach access.

## Mileages

| | |
|---|---|
| 0.0 | East Slough trailhead |
| 0.9 | Left on Gap Point Trail |
| 2.0 | Bayside Trail splits right; keep straight |
| 2.8 | Campsite 1 |
| 4.0 | Campsite 2 |
| 6.4 | East Slough trailhead |

# 6

## Apalachicola Backpack

### Overview

This backpack traverses the easterly half of the vast, wild, and demanding Apalachicola National Forest. Follow the Florida Trail along the scenic Sopchoppy River before entering unforgettable Bradwell Bay Wilderness, with its ultrachallenging swamp-slog. From there make your way west to end at Porter Lake Campground.

**Distance & Configuration**: 32.5 mile end-to-end
**Difficulty**: Difficult due to distance and Bradwell Bay Wilderness
**Outstanding Features**: Sopchoppy River, untamed wilderness
**Scenery**: 4
**Solitude**: 4
**Family-Friendly**: 0
**Canine-Friendly**: 0
**Fees/Permits**: No fees or permits required
**Best Season**: November through mid-April
**Maps**: Apalachicola National Forest
**For More Info**: Apalachicola National Forest, Wakulla Ranger District, 57 Taff Dr, Crawfordville, FL 32327, 850-926-3561, https://www.fs.usda.gov/recarea/florida/recarea/?recid=83574
**Finding the Trailhead**: To reach the Porter Lake trailhead from US 319 in Sopchoppy, take Rose Street west for 0.6 mile; then veer right onto CR 375, Smith Creek Road. Follow it for 15.6 miles and then turn left onto Forest Highway 13. Follow it for 0.6 mile to Porter Lake Campground on your left. Do not block campsites. To reach the Carraway Cutoff trailhead from Porter Lake, backtrack to Sopchoppy and then take US 319 north for 5.2 miles to turn right onto Carraway Cutoff Road. Follow it 0.1 mile to the trailhead on your left. Note: Overnight parking is not allowed at the Carraway Cutoff trailhead. Park in Sopchoppy and get a ride to the trailhead. GPS trailhead coordinates: Porter Lake: 30.176993, -84.677052; Carraway Cutoff Road: 30.075029, -84.405026

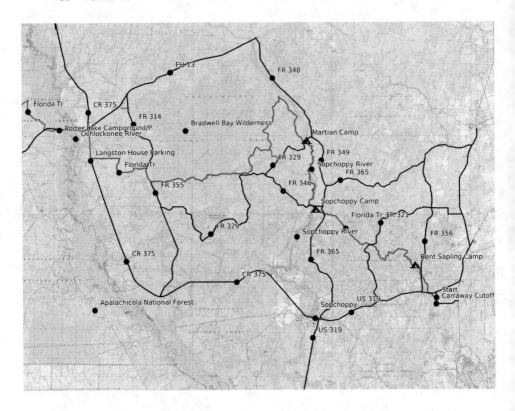

This adventurous, challenging backpack takes place in the Apalachicola National Forest, a land of scenic waterways and vast, remote forests. The Florida Trail is your conduit as you first traverse rolling pine woods to make the Sopchoppy River, meandering beneath live oaks shading the blackwater stream, lined with huge cypress trees and working around gullied tributaries. Then you tackle Bradwell Bay Wilderness where you first travel through sun-beaten scant pines rising above palmetto prairies before navigating miles of wet, cypress, and hardwood swamps with very little dry land about. Beyond the wilderness, the path remains wet, cruising through row-cropped slash pines. Finally, a little road walking leads you to Porter Lake Campground, a recommended parking area. Camping options are enhanced with designated camps set along the Florida Trail, though you can also find your own sites. No designated sites exist in Bradwell Bay Wilderness. Finding cleared, dry, level spots requires diligence. Water is abundant everywhere.

The path is mostly single-track, though it does cross and occasionally follow forest roads. This backpack leaves Carraway Cutoff Road west in piney woods to quickly cross US 319 at 0.3 mile. The single-track path enters forest

Swamp-slogging is part of backpacking the Apalachicola National Forest.

of pine, live oak, and laurel oak with lots of sparkleberry and azalea. Cross boardwalks over low areas of bay, titi, and cypress, then rise to pines. Bisect Forest Road (FR) 356 at 1.3 miles.

The next thicket, with a wide stream beneath the dark canopy, is crossed at 1.8 miles. At 1.9 miles, a blue-blazed spur trail leads right to Bent Sapling Camp. It offers limited tent sites, benches, and a fire ring under pines, turkey oaks, and brush. The Florida Trail continues through low sand hills of pine and turkey oak broken by titi thickets through which water flows. Crossing these thickets is an often wet-footed proposition, but some have plank bridges.

Cross FR 321 at 5.3 miles. The next section makes a lot of twists and turns—stay with blazes. Pass under a major transmission line at 5.5 miles. Go on and off FR 321-C. The mature pinelands ahead are favored by red-cockaded woodpeckers, as is evidenced by numerous pines circled with white paint stripes, indicating woodpecker nests.

By 7.5 miles, the Florida Trail enters an area with many live oaks and laurel oaks before dropping into low woods with many big trees. Of special note are the old-growth sweetbay magnolia trees. Commonly known as bay trees, they extend from South Florida northward to Massachusetts and westward to Texas. Also, scan for red maple and tulip poplars. Cross FR 365 at 8.3 miles and continue northwest through shady woods. At 8.7 miles, reach signed Sopchoppy Camp, with fire ring, benches, and ample tent spots under widespread oaks. Water can be had from the nearby river.

Head along the coffee-colored Sopchoppy River to reach FR 346 at 8.9 miles. Turn left on the sandy vehicle road, spanning the Sopchoppy River, and then split right into woods at a trail parking area. Head up the west bank of the Sopchoppy River in rich woods of water oak, sweetgum, red maple, and pine. You will begin a pattern of trekking riverside berms above the water, then circling around gullies feeding the river, with its impressive cypress trees. Sand live oak, palmetto, live oak, and holly border the river and trail. Undulate through cypress- and cane-filled ravines.

Leave the Sopchoppy at 10.5 miles, crossing Monkey Creek on a steel-trussed bridge at 11.0 miles. Rise to a pine plantation, returning to the Sopchoppy River at 11.5 miles, with its blooming azaleas and sparkleberry. Once more, clamber the steep ravines. Swamps border the river in places—the trail effectively straddles the bluff between the Sopchoppy and the swamps on the left.

At 13.2 miles, reach the Sopchoppy River backcountry campsite, strangely known as Martian Camp. It offers benches, flat tent sites, fire ring, and shade from nearby oaks. Ahead, reach FR 329 ahead; follow the forest road west for 0.2 mile to reach the Bradwell Bay Wilderness trailhead at 13.4 miles. Head north into the nearly 25,000-acre untamed parcel, named for a hunter who was lost for days in its swamps and thickets. This wilderness is home to black bears—you may see their acorn-laden scat on the path. Trace an old road, flanked by a canal, through mixed flatwoods. Open into a sun-splashed brush plain and then span a creek on the old road bridge at 14.4 miles under mixed oaks and pines. At 14.8 miles, enter a palmetto/gallberry plain over which the blackened trunks of pines tower. At 15.9 miles, reach a stand of live oaks on trail left. Just a short distance past the live oaks, leave the roadbed and make an acute turn left onto another, less obvious roadbed. Watch for the double blazes here. The roadbed the trail has been following continues north and crosses a creek.

The now-fainter Florida Trail keeps southwest on a brushy, pine-pocked prairie. At 16.9 miles, bisect a titi thicket through which a stream flows. Keep alternately tromping titi thickets between pine/palmetto islands. At 18.9 miles, come to an old forest road, where a spur trail leads left 0.5 mile through palmetto prairie and turkey oaks to reach FR 329 and the Monkey Creek trailhead.

The Florida Trail continues right, westerly, in pine flatwoods. Descend into a titi/cypress swamp, crossing a feeder stream of Monkey Creek at 20.0 miles. Emerge onto a palmetto plain with a few scattered pond pines and longleaf pines. The trail is brushy in spots. Drop again to ford Monkey

Creek at 20.7 miles. This may be a deep ford in high-water years. Lush forest gives way to tall longleaf woodland. At 21.3 miles, a spur trail leads left 0.1 mile to FR 329.

Descend into a wet area of bay, pond pine, and cypress. This swamp section is broken by one little area of pines at 21.9 miles. Quickly enter another unbroken swamp. The challenge is on. Overhead are old-growth trees—loblolly pine, cypress, and gum. At 23.6 miles, the stilled waters through which you walk can be quite mucky. More open sections of water can and will easily top your knees. Roots, submerged logs, and deep pockets make for uneven and rough going. Make every step count. Depending on the year's rainfall, I've been through up to my ankles and up to my waist.

At 24.6 miles, pick up a logging tram with canals on both sides of it. The dry land is open. Turn once again into swamp, still tracing the tram bed. This swamp tromp is brief, and you return to ragged pines and some wet walking before emerging on FR 314 at 25.9 miles, leaving Bradwell Bay Wilderness. Turn right and walk along the built-up forest road for 0.6 mile; then leave the forest road and turn left onto double-track through pines. The water table is quite high here, and the path will be wet in places. At 28.2 miles, the Florida Trail veers right, north, onto remote FR 388-A. Follow it for 0.6 mile to double orange blazes leaving left, west. Enter another wet pine plantation. Pass through a pine/titi/bay thicket on a side trail, avoiding deep water on the jeep road. Ahead, work around another titi/cypress thicket, keeping westerly.

Emerge onto CR 375, Smith Creek Road, at 30.0 miles. The nonrecommended Langston House parking area is across the road. Turn right and follow the paved road north over Smith Creek then turn left onto Forest Highway (FH) 13 at 31.3 miles. Turn left on FH 13, following it over the Ochlockonee River. Pass another bridge over Porter Lake and drop off the road to reach Porter Lake Campground and hike's end at 32.5 miles.

## Mileages

0.0 Carraway Cutoff Road
0.3 Cross US 319
1.0 Cross FR 365
1.9 Bent Sapling Camp
5.3 Cross FR 321
8.7 Sopchoppy Camp
11.0 Bridge Monkey Creek
13.2 Martian Camp
13.4 Enter Bradwell Bay Wilderness

| 15.9 | Sharp left in live oaks |
| 18.9 | Spur left to FR 329 |
| 20.7 | Ford Monkey Creek |
| 21.3 | Spur left to FR 329 |
| 23.6 | Still, deep heart of swamp-slog |
| 24.6 | Join logging tram |
| 25.9 | Leave wilderness; right on FR 314 |
| 26.5 | Left from FR 314 |
| 28.2 | Right on remote FR 388-A |
| 30.0 | Smith Creek Road |
| 31.3 | Left on FH 13 |
| 32.5 | Porter Lake Campground |

# 7

## Aucilla River Backpack

### Overview

This overnight adventure leads you along the peculiar but scenic Aucilla River. Take the Florida Trail north from the sinks of the Aucilla and trace its meanderings through majestic, lush hammock forests to a fine backcountry campsite. From there you can either backtrack or continue the Florida Trail to reach sand roads then loop back to the trailhead.

---

**Distance & Configuration**: 14.4-mile there-and-back or 14.9-mile loop
**Difficulty**: Moderate
**Outstanding Features**: Aucilla River, hardwood hammock forests
**Scenery**: 4
**Solitude**: 3
**Family-Friendly**: 2
**Canine-Friendly**: 4
**Fees/Permits**: No fees or permits required
**Best Season**: November through mid-April
**Maps**: Florida National Scenic Trail: Aucilla River and Sinks
**For More Info**: Florida Fish and Wildlife Commission, North Central Region, 3377 E
    US Hwy 90, Lake City, FL 32055, 386-758-0525, https://myfwc.com/
**Finding the Trailhead**: From Perry, take US 98 west for 21 miles. Then turn right
    on Powell Hammock Road and follow it for 3.5 miles. Then turn left on Goose
    Pasture Road and follow it for 1.1 miles to the Aucilla Sinks trailhead on your
    right, with a kiosk to your left. GPS trailhead coordinates: 30.200835, -83.924304

---

The Aucilla River is one of Florida's more scenic locales, for paddling, camping—and backpacking. Flowing through a karst region where water appears and disappears through underground channels, the waterway is bordered in rich hammock forest of cabbage palm, live oak, red maple, and water oaks. A segment of the Florida Trail runs through this eye-pleasing haven, with

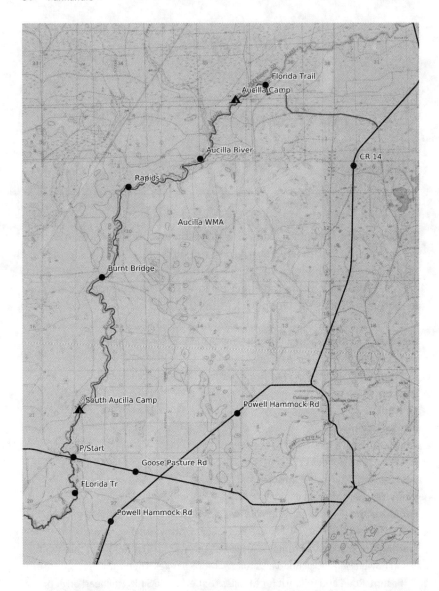

near continual river scenes as well as views of sinkholes, overflow swamps, and rock outcrops.

Backpackers can overnight at a pair of designated sites, merely level spots with no amenities. You can either treat this adventure as an out-and-back proposition, doubling your Aucilla action, or return via sand roads that present speedier hiking. The trail along the Aucilla is almost all single-track, but it does cross occasional access and forest roads running near the river.

Trek alongside the Aucilla River on this backpack.

Begin the hike by walking a few feet west on Goose Pasture Road; then head north around the west side of a sink. Note the moving water in the sink. Follow the Florida Trail north beyond the sink under junglesque woods of tall oaks, sweetgum, holly, palms, and thick underbrush. Wind past another sink. View cypresses growing from the sinks. At 0.2 mile, come to another sink known as "The Vortex" for its swirling descent into the underground at higher flows.

The Florida Trail keeps north, passing more sinks, then you saddle along the Aucilla River where it is flowing, a half mile from the trailhead. Begin coursing along the waterway as it runs dusky by rock outcrops, fallen trees, and sandbars. At 0.8 mile, hike by the smallish and not recommended South Aucilla River Camp, set directly by the water near some limestone outcrops. Continue on single-track upriver.

Moss-draped hardwoods rise high overhead. The river is close by. The trail can flood if the USGS Aucilla River at Lamont gauge is above 51 feet. Check ahead if conditions have been rainy. Note the prevalence of river birch trees, with their peeling gold trunks. In the Sunshine State, river birches are found only in North Florida and the Panhandle. At 2.1 miles, pass a river access. Ahead, in places you travel a berm above the river with an overflow swamp on the other side. These sloughs fill during floods and rains, then slowly drain back into the Aucilla, both above and below ground.

Come to Burnt Bridge at 3.3 miles. Here, to your left, a bridge once spanned the Aucilla. Nothing but shoreline supports remain. Resume up-river. At 4.8 miles, reach the Aucilla Rapids, where the waterway descends amid limestone, frothing loud. Cypress knees border the shoals. The river and trail curve northeast in gorgeous woods rich with azalea and sparkle-berry. Pass a couple of sinks away from the Aucilla.

At 7.2 miles, a blue-blazed trail splits left a short distance to Aucilla River Camp, a fine spot with river access, a grass and pine needle understory shaded by hardwoods. Camp here. The next day you can either backtrack or follow the Florida Trail a short piece along the river before it pulls away into pines and then turns east on forest roads to reach CR 14. From there, if you want to make a loop, follow CR 14 south to turn right onto Powell Hammock Road and then right again on Goose Pasture Road to the trailhead.

## Mileages

- 0.0   Goose Pasture Road
- 0.8   South Aucilla River Camp
- 3.3   Burnt Bridge
- 4.8   Aucilla Rapids
- 7.2   Aucilla River Campsite
- 14.4  Goose Pasture Road

### Set up Your Backpack Camp Like Home

Setting up a backcountry camp is like setting up your home. Think of your campsite as having a bedroom, kitchen, living room, and bathroom. Each area has its own distinctive characteristics that you will be emulating.

When setting up your sleeping quarters, try to find level ground that is not subject to water flow. Look on the ground where you plan to sleep. Do you see evidence of water running through that spot? If so, find another location. Also look for a layer of natural duff, such as leaves or pine needles, which indicates that water is not running through it—running water scours the ground. Duff pads your bedroom. Do not clear the ground before setting up your bedroom, but do look for sticks, rocks, and other obstructions that might interrupt your sleep. Hammock campers simply need two conveniently located trees.

If you like to cook over a fire as I do, your kitchen will be located near the fire ring. I will have my grill and pot located in one general area. My food will be nearby while I'm in camp, but if I leave, it will be hung up away from critters.

Backpackers expect a spartan living room. This may merely amount to a backpack leaning against a tree with a sleeping pad to sit on. That is one of the reasons I carry a closed-cell sleeping pad, because I can use it when sitting around the fire and don't have to worry about it popping as I do about an air mattress.

Additional comforts will be found in your "camp furniture." Backpackers have to take what they can find in the natural surroundings for their camp furniture, though these days some backpackers (including myself) carry ultralight folding camp chairs. At already established sites, you often find a combination of logs creating a bench of sorts. Land managers often place metal fire grates, picnic tables, and/or wooden benches at designated campsites.

When looking for a campsite, consider the camp furniture, not only for yourself but also your belongings. Satellite logs and stumps can act as tables for your cook set and other gear you might prefer not to set on the ground.

The campsite bathroom should be well away from the other parts of camp. When using the bathroom, head away from camp and away from any water source and find a concealed location. Dig a hole using a stick or the heel of your shoe, preferably 6 inches deep, do your business, burn your toilet paper, and then cover it up.

Backpackers should consider whether to set up a base camp or keep moving day-to-day. A base camp frees you from the chores of setting up and breaking down camp on a daily basis, availing more free time and fewer camp chores.

The advantage of moving camp on a daily basis is that you will be setting up in new surroundings every day. This allows for convenient sightseeing from each campsite. If you are going on a long backpacking adventure, consider staying at one camp for two nights during the middle of the trip just to free you from the daily making/breaking camp ritual. So whether you go for one night or ten, make your backpacking camp resemble home.

# North Florida

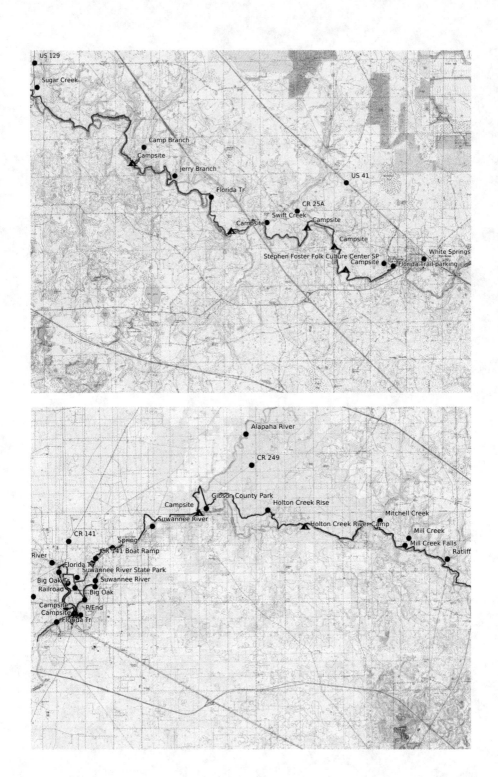

# 8

## Suwannee River Backpack

### Overview

This 50-plus-mile, end-to-end Florida Trail backpack travels along Florida's contribution to great rivers of the world—the Suwannee—traversing gorgeous woodlands perched along the banks of the waterway, passing sandbars, clear springs, wooded overflow swamps, as well as hills and bluffs that offer some of the most scenic backpacking in the Sunshine State. The adventure begins at Stephen Foster Folk Culture Center State Park and traces the Suwannee downstream on mostly public lands that avail good and varied camping opportunities, to end at Suwannee River State Park.

**Distance & Configuration**: 50.9-mile end-to-end

**Difficulty**: Difficult due to distance

**Outstanding Features**: River scenes, good campsites, long-distance opportunity

**Scenery**: 5

**Solitude**: 3

**Family-Friendly**: 1

**Canine-Friendly**: 2

**Fees/Permits**: Parking fees required at both ends of the trail.

**Best season**: November through late April

**Maps**: Suwannee River Wilderness Trail Paddling Guide—maps 2 through 17

**For more info**: Suwannee River Wilderness State Trail, 4298 NW CR 292, Mayo, FL 32066, 800-868-9914, https://www.floridastateparks.org/

**Finding the Trailhead**: To reach the Suwannee River State Park trailhead from Live Oak, drive west on US 90 for 12.2 miles to turn right into the state park, reaching the entrance station. Ask for the latest overnight parking location. To reach the backpack's beginning, backtrack to Live Oak, then turn left, north, on US 129 and follow it just a short distance, turning right on FL 136, Duval Street. Stay with it 14.3 miles to the town of White Springs and US 41. Turn left on US 41 north and follow it 0.1 mile to turn left on Lillian Sanders Drive, entering

Stephen Foster Folk Culture Center State Park. Follow the signs to the River Gazebo and overnight parking. GPS trailhead coordinates: Suwannee River State Park: 30.383047, -83.167290, Stephen Foster Culture Center State Park: 30.329372, -82.767247

---

Many Florida backpackers declare this Suwannee River adventure to be Florida's best overnight endeavor. It is certainly in the top ten. The scenery is simply first-rate: bluff views of the Suwannee, huge live oaks rising from wooded overflow swamps, white lilies coloring leafy forest floors, clear surging springs, limestone cliffs and bluffs, bona fide waterfalls where tributaries plunge into the Suwannee River, shadowy wooded swamps, distant views from bluffs, and hills that will get your heartbeat thumpin'.

A couple of items right off: Don't let the 50-mile distance deter you. It can easily be shortened or sectioned off. Despite being an end-to-end trek, the logistics are easily solved. For starters, state parks at each end offer safe, fee parking. Furthermore, area outfitters—mostly serving Suwannee River paddlers—will also shuttle Florida Trail backpackers starting about anywhere you want. However, I highly recommend the entire enchilada. Along the way, the hike travels Suwannee River Water Management District (SRWMD) lands that offer camping, including designated established campsites, even a wilderness camp presenting water, screen shelters, and showers! You can also overnight on riverside sandbars if you choose, as well as execute dispersed camping on SRWMD lands. Try to use designated, established campsites where possible. The state parks on either end also avail auto-accessible camping before or after your trip.

While backpacking you will also follow roads for short periods and cross private property open to the public, including riverside houses. These private lands are interspersed with SRWMD lands. The entire route—part of the Florida Trail—is clearly blazed throughout, including the road sections. Stay with the blazes and you'll be fine. Please show respect for the landowners while traveling through private lands.

Much of the hike traverses wooded berms above the Suwannee River, created when the river overflows it banks. To your left will be the river below, and to your right will be overflow swamp forests where live oaks grow to huge sizes, draped in Spanish moss and complemented by sweetgum, river birch, palmetto, ferns, and beard cane. Sparkleberry, holly, and laurel oak also find their place while you circle fertile side valleys where lesser blackwater streams contribute their flows to the Suwannee. The pathway is continually undulating up and down, adding challenge. The Suwannee River Wilderness Trail Paddling Guide is a downloadable comprehensive

Backpack past waterfalls on the Suwannee River Backpack.

map book that not only shows river and land features but also the Florida Trail as it travels along the Suwannee. This map book is indispensable for a Suwannee River backpack.

The following is a mile-by-mile trail log to make your adventure happen on this exciting yet challenging long-distance backpack.

## Mileages

0.0  Leave from the River Gazebo parking area at Stephen Foster Folk Culture Center State Park, descending a boardwalk toward the river. Soon reach terra firma. Head right, downstream along the Suwannee River, tracing the orange blazes of the Florida Trail.

0.2  Cross the state park paddler access road.

2.0  Reach a designated campsite, with picnic table, fire ring, and benches in pines and hardwoods on a bluff well above the river. Continue on a bluff above the river.

2.7  View limestone bluffs as you curve with the river. Work around private land.

3.0  Campsite with seats and fire rings above the river. Florida Trail next works around private lands away from the water; hike north, bridging Sal Marie Branch, then turn westerly on a sand road, parallel to CR 25A.

4.5  Split left on a double-track back to SRWMD lands, Swift Creek Tract.

4.7  Reach a good designated campsite with fire ring and benches in open area bordered by live oaks above the river. Private property nearby. Continue south along Suwannee River. Alternately travel through palmetto thickets overlorded by oaks and pines as well as beside the river on a berm. Terrain is hilly.

6.9  Bridge gorgeous limestone-bordered Swift Creek on a trail bridge as it speeds toward the Suwannee River. Continue in hilly terrain, passing under a power line ahead.

7.3  Hike under the twin bridges of noisy I-75 after undulating past a small stream. Resume downriver, now in the Jerry Branch Tract.

8.2  Reach a designated campsite on a bluff above the Suwannee with a fire ring in a mix of oaks and pines.

9.7  Turn west, bisecting a sharp bend in the river.

10.7  Step over a narrow gully and then resume along the river.

11.0  Reach a steep hilly area while working around the outside of a bend in the river.

11.6  Bridge pretty Jerry Branch. Stay in hilly terrain. Magnolias become common.

12.5  Climb steps ascending to a bluff. Work around steep ravines.

13.7  Come to an intersection. Here, a spur trail leads right to a campsite and connector trails looping up Camp Branch. The smallish campsite, with benches and fire ring, is situated above the streambed of Camp Branch. Ahead, the Florida Trail takes you by the river in front of private houses. Stay with the blazes.

15.4 Cross a tumbling branch and then begin some of Florida's hilliest hiking—the Devils Mountain.

16.7 Enter the SRWMD's Sugar Creek Tract. Work around some sinks and shortcut a bend. Keep along the river, enjoying good water views directly alongside the limestone-lined waterway.

17.0 Shortcut another river bend; this bend is very sharp.

17.4 Curve on the inside of a bend directly above an accessible sandbar, keep westerly, working around a wooded ravine.

17.9 Leave the river.

19.1 Briefly return to the water after passing under a massive power line. Ahead, pass under a graffiti-blotched abandoned train bridge.

19.7 Pass under US 129 and then join SW 79th Terrace. Walk west on the sand road. Ahead the trail becomes more primitive.

21.1 Return to the river on foot track. Shortly pass the remains of an old, abandoned railroad bridge. Cedars become more prevalent in the woods.

21.6 Hop over Ratliff Branch. Continue on beautiful bluffs. Look for occasional trail-accessible sandbars on this side of the river.

23.6 Cross Mill Creek above a two-tier waterfall tumbling over limestone before entering the Suwannee River. Climb to pass a lone dwelling. Sinks are common in the woods. Watch for big live oaks in this area.

25.0 Bridge Mitchell Creek. You are now in the large Holton Creek Tract. Savor the remote atmosphere of the Tract. Hike along the river berm as well.

27.4 Cut through a small riverside inholding. Soon return to riverside hiking. Massive live oaks can be found in sight of the trail.

28.0 Hike above a riverside spring that is difficult to reach.

29.1 Come to Holton Creek River Camp, with reservable screen shelters, tent campsites with fire ring, picnic shelter, electrical outlets, water, and hot showers, primarily used by paddlers. Continue west along the north bank of the Suwannee River.

30.2 Turn away from the Suwannee River, aiming north for Holton Creek Rise in big palmetto-cloaked sinks. Come along Holton Creek.

31.3 Circle around the north side of dark Holton Creek Rise, potential campsites hereabouts. A blue-blazed spur trail leads right to alternate access. Head westerly, well back from the Suwannee River in beautiful forests.

34.4 Pop out on CR 751, just north of Gibson Park, with water, boat ramp, picnic shelter, electrical outlets, and auto-accessible camping. Head right, north, away from Gibson County Park, continuing north on CR 751.

35.1 Split left into woods after bridging the Alapaha River; resume single-track trail following the Alapaha River downstream.

35.5 Sandbar on inside of bend in Alapaha River.

36.4 Spur trail goes left to good campsite with fire ring, benches, and sandbar above the confluence of the Alapaha and Suwannee Rivers; Florida Trail heads west on sand SW 69th Way, then turns left back into woods.

37.6 Return to river's edge in hickory, oak, and pine woods.

38.2 Leave northwest from Suwannee River again.

38.7 Turn south after coming along road, reenter full-blown woods in SRWMD Jones Spring Tract. Ahead, circle around a sink.

39.3 Return to river's edge, tracing the Suwannee downstream.

39.6 Pop out at intersection of Maiden Lane and SW Armor Blvd, both sand roads. Stay west with blazed Florida Trail on a grassy track.

39.7 Head south back into woods, soon entering Suwannee River State Park.

39.9 Cut across a bend in the river.

41.0 The Florida Trail travels above an accessible clear spring set against the riverbank.

41.7 Pop out on a road next to a trailer community. Stay left on a sand road.

41.9 Split left to CR 141 boat ramp. Go through fence and reenter Suwannee River State Park.

42.4 A spur trail goes right; stay left along river with the Florida Trail.

44.1 The Big Oak Trail goes right. A huge oak tree is just a short distance up the path. Resume the Florida Trail along the river. The primary state park nature trail network is across the river. Cut across a big gas line clearing.

44.9 Come to a good designated campsite at the confluence of the Suwannee and Withlacoochee Rivers. Hike's end is just across the Suwannee River, but you have miles to go. Turn north up the right bank of the Withlacoochee River, now heading upstream on wooded bluffs.

46.7 Head right, east, from the Withlacoochee, staying inside state park bounds on a wide, grassy track.

47.0 Head left, north, on a blazed right-of-way after crossing the gas line clearing again. Work around private land.

47.5 Reach paved CR 141. Head left, bridging the Withlacoochee River; then turn south, backing into woods downstream along the Withlacoochee in pine-dominated woods.

49.1 Come alongside Florida Gulf & Atlantic Railroad.

49.9 Reach a campsite and trail intersection on a bluff above dark Suwanacoochee Spring. Head west, pass under railroad tracks, and then enter Ellaville's Dupont Park, with picnic tables. The main Florida Trail heads left, continuing down the Suwannee River. Cut through the park and join old US 90 across graffiti splattered Hillman Bridge, crossing the Suwannee River.

50.4 Split left on River Road just after passing a Florida agricultural inspection station. Follow River Road and cross railroad tracks. Just after that, split left on the historic Earthworks Trail.

50.9 Pop out near a picnic shelter and the main parking area of Suwannee River State Park, completing the exciting backpack.

# 9

## Osceola Backpack

### Overview

Travel through the wild—and wet—woods of the Osceola National Forest with the one and only Florida Trail as your conduit. Begin at fine Ocean Pond Campground and then work northwest in a deep pine world floored by saw palmetto. End your first day at a high-and-dry trail shelter. The next day continue past the Turkey Run trailhead through untamed flatwoods to make an oak refuge and camp near West Tower Hunt Camp. The final part of the adventure winds to the forest's west boundary after tunneling beneath increasing oak woods to end at the Deep Creek trailhead.

---

**Distance & Configuration**: 16.3 mile end-to-end
**Difficulty**: Moderate, but trail is rugged and wet
**Outstanding Features**: Vast forests, trail shelter
**Scenery**: 3
**Solitude**: 4
**Family-Friendly**: 2
**Canine-Friendly**: 2
**Fees/Permits**: No fees or permit required
**Best Season**: Late October through late April
**Maps**: Osceola National Forest
**For More Info**: Osceola National Forest, 24874 US Hwy 90, Sanderson, FL 32087, 386-752-2577, https://www.fs.usda.gov/
**Finding the Trailhead**: To reach backpack's end and Deep Creek trailhead from exit 303 on I-10 north of Lake City, take US 441 north for 7.6 miles to turn right onto NE Drew Road. Follow it 0.8 mile to the signed Deep Creek trailhead on your right. To reach the backpack's starting point, backtrack to US 441 and take it south for 9.9 miles to turn left onto paved CR 250, Gum Swamp Road. Follow it 11 miles to turn right onto paved CR 250A and follow it for 3.3 miles. Then follow the entrance road into Ocean Pond Campground. Contact a campground

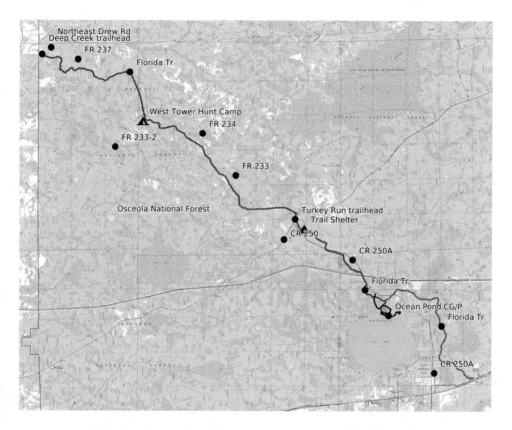

host about exact parking. Pick up the Florida Trail connector just a little west of the campground entrance station, at the far end of the dump station turnaround. GPS trailhead coordinates: Deep Creek trailhead 30.348842, -82.607784, Ocean Pond trailhead 30.240151, -82.435274

The Osceola National Forest is often overlooked as a backpacking destination. It has no singular highlights, is often wet, and has a sameness of flora. Yet it is a vast tract of untamed Florida that presents a backpacking opportunity that I've enjoyed time and again over the years. The attraction for me—trekking through a large expanse of eye-pleasing forest, which becomes harder and harder to find as Florida's population grows.

The backpack as laid out is good as well, with a great starting point in Ocean Pond Campground and a good ending spot at Deep Creek trailhead. With two primary overnighting spots along the way, you can make an easy two-nighter or a moderate one-night trip. The trail is well marked and maintained, albeit wet. Bring extra camp shoes because your hiking shoes

Spend the night at this evergreen-enveloped trail shelter.

will get wet. You can find other campsites if you look hard (the underbrush is often thick), especially near trail's end at Deep Creek, among stately oaks.

The backpack begins on a trail connecting Ocean Pond Campground to the Florida Trail. Leave the west side of the Ocean Pond RV dump station on a blue-blazed track heading west along the edge of the highly recommended campground. At 0.1 mile, cross the first of many boardwalks spanning small streams gurgling through titi thickets; then cross the paved campground entrance road at 0.3 mile. The connector turns northeast to meet the Florida Trail at 0.5 mile in an often-wet trail junction. Head left, westbound, most likely sloshing along in normal to wet years. Overhead, pines stretch as far as the eye can see while in the near bay trees and palmetto fashion a thick understory. Palmetto shrubs grow throughout the Osceola National Forest. It is the most easily recognizable shrub in the state, with fan-shaped leaves growing from an oft-buried trunk. Palmettos grow in a wide variety of conditions, including sandy prairies, dunes, palm hammocks, and flatwoods such as these. Palmetto ranges up the east coast into Georgia and the Carolinas and is the northernmost-growing palm in North America. The leaves were once used for making baskets, brooms, and hats.

Cross the campground entrance road a second time and then ramble through woods and traipse boardwalks among cypress stands. Emerge onto

Forest Road (FR) 241, then turn right and join paved CR 250A left at 1.5 miles, spanning busy I-10, providing unadorned contrast to your backpacking experience. Return left to woods at 1.9 miles, beginning a long stretch of pine flatwoods. At 3.4 miles, the trail pops out on CR 250A. Turn left and follow the paved road to bridge a creek via road; then head north, back into pines. Ahead, turn west in classic pine flatwoods. At 4.4 miles, bridge a canal and then turn right, coming to a tin-roofed, open-sided trail shelter with outside fire ring. The adjacent canal provides water. Small tent sites are carved from the woods. This is a recommended first night's destination.

Keep northwest beyond the shelter in pines to emerge at paved CR 250 and the Turkey Run trailhead at 4.8 miles. The Florida Trail works northwest in the driest woods around, sometimes joining a double-track. At 5.8 miles, bisect a cypress strand. You will often hike along the perimeter of cypress strands and pine woods, then cross the strand, sometimes on boardwalks, like at 6.7, 6.9, and 7.1 miles. Note the pines and cypress growing in the same area. The pines here are buttressed at their base, indicating occasional inundation. Go on and off double-track. Stay with the blazes. Cut through a palmetto prairie, crossing Forest Road (FR) 234-1 at 9.2 miles.

Enter dense pines. Cross a significant stream via boardwalk at 10.3 miles. More boardwalks lie ahead. At 11.4 miles, look for blue blazes and a sand forest road leading left to West Tower Hunt Camp. After just a short distance on the spur, come to a fine campsite in oaks. The main hunt camp, with a faucet, is beyond. From here, the Florida Trail aims more northerly, joining an elevated logging tram to cross FR 233 at 11.5 miles. The berm leads you through a wetter cypress-pine wood. Look for crossties embedded in the berm. Several boardwalks lead over old canals.

At 12.7 miles, the Florida Trail splits left onto a double-track, heading westerly through pine flatwoods. At 13.6 miles, the route splits right, back onto single-track. Oaks increase in number and create cleared flats with potential camping, without easily available water. At 14.6 miles, cross FR 237. Keep winding westerly, working through more oak-dominated, drier wood. Stay with the blazes to emerge at Deep Creek trailhead on Northeast Drew Road, just across from a house, at 16.3 miles, completing the linear backpack.

## Mileages

0.0   Ocean Pond trailhead
0.5   Join Florida Trail
4.4   Trail shelter, campsite
4.8   Turkey Run trailhead
9.2   Cross FR 234-1
11.4   Spur left to West Tower Hunt Camp, campsites
14.6   Cross FR 237
16.3   Deep Creek trailhead

# 10

## Saint Marys Backpack

### Overview

This fine circuit trek leads you through Ralph E. Simmons State Forest to a pair of quality backcountry campsites situated on the scenic Saint Marys River. The riverside campsites are a treat. Along the way you will past pine/wiregrass uplands, along with cypress swamps and low evergreen forests.

---

**Distance & Configuration**: 7.8-mile loop
**Difficulty**: Easy
**Outstanding Features**: Outstanding campsites, good trail conditions
**Scenery**: 5
**Solitude**: 3
**Family-Friendly**: 4
**Canine-Friendly**: 4
**Fees/Permits**: No fees or permits required
**Best Season**: Late October through April
**Maps**: Ralph E. Simmons Memorial State Forest
**For More Info**: Ralph E. Simmons State Forest, 3742 Clint Dr, Hilliard, FL 32046, 904-845-4933, https://www.fdacs.gov/
**Finding the Trailhead**: From the intersection of US 1 and SR A1A in Callahan, head north on US 1 for 17.8 miles to Lake Hampton Road, just before the US 1 bridge over the Saint Marys River. Ignore signs for Ralph E. Simmons State Forest until you reach Lake Hampton Road. Turn right on Lake Hampton Road and follow it for 2.5 miles to Penny Haddock Road. Turn left on Penny Haddock Road and follow it for 0.8 mile; then veer left into the trailhead parking area. GPS trailhead coordinates: 30.794080, -81.938391

---

Ralph E. Simmons State Forest is an underrated Florida gem. The 3,600-acre preserve is located in the Saint Marys River valley, where the river forms the state boundary with Georgia. Elevations vary, helping to fashion distinctive natural communities. The river borders the forest on two sides, adding

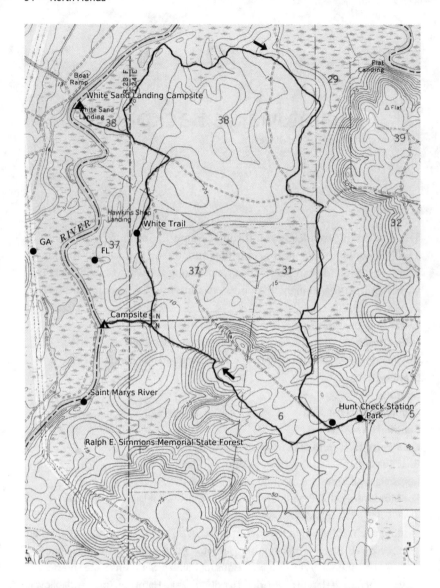

scenic value. Our loop traces the White Trail as it tours the forest. The two campsites are accessed via spur trails. Each camp presents a picnic table, fire ring, and ample tent sites. Water can be had from the river or nearby swamps.

The first campsite encountered has no name. It is set on a wooded bluff above the river, but it has a short spur accessing the river. The river landing is small and obscure, thus is seldom accessed from the Saint Marys River. If you prefer seclusion, seek this campsite. White Sand Landing Campsite

Hike through pine flatwoods en route to the alluring Saint Marys River.

is more popular, an attractive level area under big live oaks. It looks out on the river with a fine beach and water access. Be forewarned: on nice warm weekends, river boaters can congregate here.

Overall, the backpacking experience at Ralph E. Simmons State Forest is a good one, from the well-tended trail system, to the riverside campsites, to open pine flatwoods, to crowded swamp hardwoods thick with ferns and cane, to river scenes.

The White Trail leaves the trailhead, at 70 feet elevation, west on a double-track under turkey oaks and pines with a wiregrass understory. At 0.1 mile, come to a hunter check station and the loop portion of the backpack. Head left, still westbound. To your left, seepage slopes drop to a slow-moving tributary of the Saint Marys River. Stay with the white blazes as unblazed forest roads spur off the trail. At 1.0 miles, the White Trail drops into swamp woods, leaving the piney uplands. Bay trees, gum, ferns, beard cane, and sweetgum border the trail. At 1.5 miles, take the spur left to the first campsite, tracing the blue blazes west on a dry-ground peninsula bordered by wooded swamps. Reach the recommended campsite at 1.8 miles. You are just above the river, partly screened by vegetation.

Backtrack from the campsite and return to the main loop, turning left, north, into row-cropped pines. Bridge a swamp stream by culvert at 2.2 miles. At 3.0 miles, reach a "T" intersection. The White Trail heads left, west again. At 3.3 miles, split left on the elevated spur to White Sand Landing. Cypress and gum swamps border the track. Emerge on the Saint Marys River at White Sand Landing Campsite at 3.6 miles. You could throw a rock to Georgia from here.

Backtrack to the main loop and keep north, running the margin between swamps to your left and drier forest to your right. At 4.6 miles, curve away from the river, staying in low evergreen woods with thickets of palmetto. Cross a swamp of red maple, gum, and widely buttressed pines. At 5.3 miles, the trail crosses an elevated closed forest road. Continue roughly paralleling the river. Turn south in bottoms with a grassy understory and palms. At 6.0 miles, the trail follows elevated forest roads above swamps. Stay with the blazes. At 7.2 miles, cross a small swamp stream on a plank. From there you gently ascend to pines and wiregrass, completing the loop at 7.7 miles. From there it is but 0.1 mile to the trailhead.

## Mileages

0.0   Penny Haddock Road trailhead
1.8   First campsite
3.6   White Sand Landing Campsite
7.8   Penny Haddock Road trailhead

### Choose Your Backpacking Footwear Wisely

My friend Ark Evans and I were backpacking the Florida Trail Apalachicola National Forest. A slow-moving winter storm dumped inches of rain on us, raising area streams to scary heights.

The next day we came to Hickory Branch, a black-flowing charge of power. My impatience clouded my sanity, and we hiked forward, trying to ford the swollen stream. I pushed through to my waist, then backed up and decided to make a go with my pack over my head. I went forward, and the chill water went up to my chest, and the current nearly swept me off my feet. I backtracked to higher ground, minus a shoe. Once back to dry ground, we inventoried our situation and beelined to the nearest forest road, me hiking in camp sandals. Wrong shoes, wrong place.

Another time I was embarking on a backpack in Georgia's Cohutta Wilderness. The early fall skies promised a good trip. Hiking pal John Cox and I took the Hickory Creek Trail, aiming for Jacks River. I hadn't made a quarter mile in my brand-new boots when my heels started heating up. Uh, oh.

A mile farther, I was limping and asking John for Band-Aids. We cut the day short, camping on small creek. By the time we reached Jacks River the next day my heels resembled hamburger meat. I was relegated to barefoot fire tender while John did the camp chores. Next day, I hobbled to the nearest trailhead while John got the car and picked me up. Right shoes, bad fit.

When dropping a significant amount of hard-earned dough on a boot, consider having them fitted by professionals at outdoor stores. Fit is more important than brand name or shoe type or numerical shoe size.

When choosing backpacking footwear, consider the typical terrain through which you hike. Are the trails underwater much of the time? Are the trails irregular, or are they smooth and widely graded? Many backpackers can get away with low-top hiking shoes if the trails are foot friendly and their pack is light. However, if you don't have strong ankles as I do, go with shoes that give ankle support, especially when factoring in pack weight. If the trail is rough, consider additional support, using boots with a metal shank in them and a more rugged sole. If backpacking north in the Appalachians, heavier boots are preferable in winter, for warmth and snow protection.

Backpackers have a dilemma when considering footwear. They desire shoes that will support a fully loaded backpack while hiking and also are comfortable in camp. Having two pairs of shoes on your person during a backpacking trip adds weight, though camp shoes, such as flip-flops, get lighter all the time. If you are going to do a lot of hiking or going on a very long trip, I strongly recommend having quality trail shoes with quality sole. And if you find a brand that works for you, stick with that brand.

When backpacking you literally carry your own weight so you live with your decisions, for better or worse. Remember, a successful backpacking adventure starts from the ground up—with your shoes.

# 11

## North Fork Backpack

### Overview

Experience numerous natural environments on this one-night loop in Jennings State Forest. Leave the fine trailhead, then come along scenic Sweetwater Creek. Pass rich bottoms and then detour to North Fork Black Creek to camp in live oaks. Next day, curve into piney sandhills to complete the backpack.

**Distance & Configuration**: 5.2-mile loop
**Difficulty**: Easy
**Outstanding Features**: Ecosystem variety, good reservable campsite
**Scenery**: 5
**Solitude**: 2
**Family-Friendly**: 5
**Canine-Friendly**: 4
**Fees/Permits**: Parking and campsite fee required
**Best Season**: Late October through April
**Maps**: Jennings State Forest
**For More Info**: Jennings State Forest, 1337 Longhorn Rd, Middleburg, FL 32068, 904-406-6390, https://www.fdacs.gov/; Camping reservations: https://floridastateforests.reserveamerica.com/, 877-879-3859
**Finding the Trailhead**: From exit 12 on I-295 southwest of downtown, take Blanding Boulevard, FL 21, south for 8 miles to Old Jennings Road. Turn right onto Old Jennings Road and follow it for 4.1 miles nearly to a dead end; then turn right on Live Oak Road, a sand road. Follow it for 0.5 mile to reach the Old Jennings trailhead on your left. GPS trailhead coordinates: 30.122240, -81.882394

This backpack presents a fine trailhead, visual variety on the trail, and a good campsite, all situated in the 23,000-acre Jennings State Forest southwest of Jacksonville. A great backpack for families or beginners, the trail system is well marked and maintained, though it does share the trail for

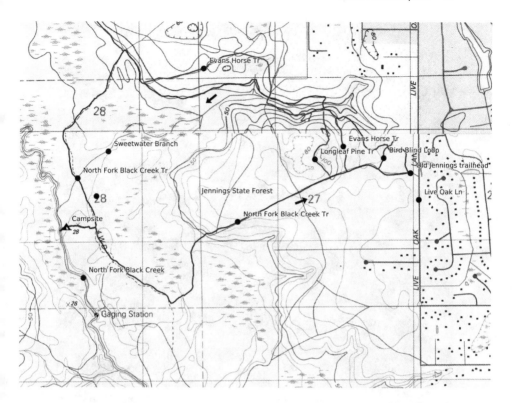

a short distance with equestrians. The two backcountry campsites (in one location) are reservable online. Along the way you will enjoy a mosaic of environments ranging from cypress and bay strands along the creek and river to open pine flatwoods to stands of turkey oak and live oak as well as streamside slope forests. The campsite offers picnic table, fire ring, and tent pads. Water can be had from North Fork Black Creek.

Start the adventure at Old Jennings trailhead, with picnic tables, restroom, water, and interpretive information in a pretty little setting. From the north side of the Old Jennings trailhead parking area, near the trailhead kiosk, look for the sign heading right, north, indicating North Fork Black Creek Trail. Your return route leaves left, westerly. Immediately enter scattered pines. At 0.1 mile, the North Fork Black Creek Trail curves left, westerly, in a mixed forest of live oak, palmetto, and pine. At 0.3 mile, reach a trail junction. Here, a spur trail leads right to a wildlife viewing blind. The Bird Blind Loop heads left, and this backpack keeps straight, running in conjunction with the Longleaf Loop. Sandhills rise to your left while you hike pine/palmetto woods with the slope of Sweetwater Branch falling to your right.

Hiking the margin between pines and cedar swamps.

At 0.6 mile, meet the Evans Horse Loop. The horse and hiking trail run in conjunction. The sand trailbed is softer here. At 0.8 mile, reach a four-way trail junction. The Longleaf Loop heads left. The Evans Horse Loop keeps straight, and this backpack turns right, diving into swamp woods concealing Sweetwater Branch. Shortly bridge the brooding yet swift sand-bottomed stream and then climb to turkey oaks. Hike west along the margin where the swamp woods and turkey oaks amalgamate. Listen as Sweetwater

Branch gurgles around cypress knees while pushing for North Fork Black Creek, as well as frogs croaking in the bordering wetlands.

At 1.0 mile, keep forward as the Evans Horse Trail crosses north. At 1.2 miles, step over a seep flowing toward Sweetwater Branch. During rainy times you may have to wade or take your shoes off here. Continue hiking parallel to Sweetwater Branch to intersect the horse trail again at 1.7 miles. The North Fork Trail and Evans Horse Trail run in conjunction for the next 0.2 mile. At 1.9 miles, reach an intersection near a gate. Here, head left with the now hiker-only North Fork Trail as the horse trail keeps straight. Enter red maple–rich bottomland forest rising over beard cane. The trail may be muddy or partially submerged here.

At 2.6 miles, a boardwalk bridge leads you across Sweetwater Branch. Rise to join the campsite spur at 2.8 miles. Reach the backcountry camp at 3.0 miles, set in a mix of open areas and shady live oaks. The path continues beyond the campsite to reach North Fork Black Creek, ensconced in thick woods. Sweetwater Branch comes in just upstream.

Next day, backtrack and rejoin the main loop, southbound. At 3.7 miles, cross a small branch of North Fork. From there, the trail rises into pine/wiregrass sandhills. Open sky can cook the path here, leaving the sandy trailbed loose, slowing your progress. At 4.8 miles, the Longleaf Pine Trail enters on your left. Stay straight, soon passing the Evans Horse Trail. Drop off the hill, then pass the Bird Blind Loop, and at 5.2 miles you are back at the trailhead.

## Mileages

0.0  Old Jennings trailhead
2.8  Spur to campsite
3.0  Campsite
5.2  Old Jennings trailhead

# 12

## Bayard Backpack

### Overview

Make an overnight loop in this valuable and picturesque tract in the shadow of Jacksonville. Take wide, easy trails through an expansive woodland to camp under live oaks on the shores of the lake-like St. Johns River. Solitude seekers have an alternate campsite choice. Your return trip traverses a variety of habitats.

---

**Distance & Configuration**: 7.1-mile loop with spur to campsite
**Difficulty**: Easy
**Outstanding Features**: Lakeside camp, well-marked and -maintained trails
**Scenery**: 4
**Solitude**: 2
**Family-Friendly**: 4
**Canine-Friendly**: 4
**Fees/permits**: No fees or permit required
**Best Season**: November through early April
**Maps**: Bayard Conservation Area
**For More Info**: St. Johns Water Management District, 4049 Reid St, Palatka, FL 32177, 386-329-4500, https://www.sjrwmd.com/
**Finding the Trailhead**: From exit 323 on I-95 northwest of St. Augustine, take International Golf Parkway west for 2.5 miles. Turn right on FL 16 west and stay with it for 10 miles. Watch ahead just after crossing the Shands Bridge over the St. Johns River. You will quickly pass Susan Drive and Shands Pier Drive on your right; you will reach the left turn into Bayard just after Shands Pier Drive. Follow the entrance road about 100 yards south; the parking will be on your left. GPS trailhead coordinates: 29.975145, -81.639291

---

Bayard Conservation Area protects a whopping 7 miles of the St. Johns River shoreline just south of Jacksonville. Almost 10,000 acres in size, the tract, managed by the St. Johns Water Management District, is worth a

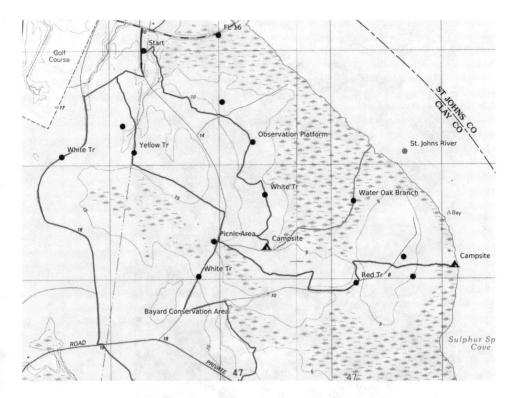

fortune—and more. Luckily for us, the tract, an important water filtration and recharge zone, is open to the public for hiking, hunting, bicycling—and backpacking.

Bayard presents two first-come, first-served campsites, one far more popular than the other. The inland site is closer to the trailhead and offers a picnic table, fire ring, and tent sites under the shelter of oaks. I recommend bringing your own water here, but Water Oak Branch flows near the campsite. It may cease flowing during drier times. The other site, the one on the shore of the St. Johns River, is a gem of a camp. It is in a waterside flat roofed over with live oaks. A light screen of cypress trees lies between you and the wide waterway. Water can be filtered from the St. Johns if you don't want to carry your own.

The hike there isn't too bad, either. The route uses a series of groomed double-track trails passing a wildlife observation platform, the first campsite, then a picnic/resting area before leading to the St. Johns River Campsite. Leave the newer parking area (moved after FL 16 was enlarged and rerouted), heading east on the White Trail in mixed woods of magnolia, oak, and pine. Stay with the blazes; some road/trails you will see aren't blazed and aren't the trail.

Campsite view of the St. Johns River.

Wander beside a palmetto prairie before reaching an elevated wildlife observation platform at 1.0 mile. Here, you can climb the tower and scan below for deer and other mammals. Wildlife observation requires patience. You have to plant yourself awhile and let wildlife come to you. Beyond the platform, the White Trail continues, reaching the left spur to the first campsite at 1.7 miles. Look for a tent symbol at the intersection. The fine campsite, reached at 1.8 miles, has a grassy base shaded by oaks and pines. Water Oak Branch flows nearby.

Backtrack from the first camp and resume the backpack, turning west to reach a substantial road, open only to water management personnel. Follow the blazes left to bridge Water Oak Branch and then, at 2.1 miles, come to a backwoods picnic area, replete with restroom, picnic table, and pump well. From the picnic area, find the Red Trail and follow it easterly, traveling through young pines, then into shady laurel oaks, sweetgum, and more mature pine. At 2.8 miles, the Red Trail hops on an elevated grassy road to bridge a swamp stream by culvert. Keep east, tracing the blazes you emerge at the St. Johns River and the large campsite overlooking the water at 3.8 miles. Most of the camp is shaded by live oaks draped in swaying Spanish moss. A broken line of cypress allows you to enjoy dramatic aquatic views from this fine camp. A small landing is nearby, but the camp doesn't appear to be overly used by motorboaters.

Backtrack, reaching the backwoods picnic area at 5.5 miles, then head north, joining the wide and easy Yellow Trail in pine-dominated mixed woods. At 7.0 miles, the Yellow Trail ends. Head right at this "T" intersection and leave right on the White Trail. The white blazes soon lead you to the south end of the large parking lot and picnic area, shaded by magnolias, ending the backpack at 7.1 miles.

## Mileages

0.0   Parking area
1.8   First campsite
2.1   Backwoods picnic area
3.8   St. Johns River Campsite
5.5   Backwoods picnic area
7.1   Parking area

### Outfitting Your Backpacker Kitchen

Backcountry cooks, since they are transporting their food and cooking implements on their back, must judiciously factor weight and space. My backpack always contains a small grill, a titanium pot that I do not mind putting over the fire, a pot grabber, tongs, a small knife, and a titanium spoon. Sometimes I tote an aluminum frying pan when cooking pancakes or fish. Don't forget the spatula!

If two or more of you are backpacking together, then y'all can split the cooking items: one takes the grill, another takes the frying pan, and still another carries the pot. Aluminum pie tins make for great lightweight and reusable plates.

Don't be afraid to tweak your cook kit for different seasons and circumstances. For example, if you were going on a long-distance Florida Trail backpack, you might want to pare down your cook kit, whereas a relaxing, shorter distance trip you can bring the extras and engage in some serious campfire cookery.

Consider the following items for your backpacking adventure:

**Camp stove**: Backpacking camp stoves range from white gas models with tanks to those with canisters and a whole cook kit built around the stove. All backcountry models should be single burner. Stoves using canisters can be problematic, since unless you are using a brand-new canister you never know exactly how much fuel is in the canister. Therefore, I recommend stoves using white gas. Alcohol stoves are very lightweight and use less fuel, but backpackers are limited by the energy output of the alcohol stove. Alcohol stoves can boil water for coffee or reconstituting a freeze-dried meal, but forget any actual cooking over them.

**Cook Kit**: Cook kits come in a wide variety of sizes and weights, from nearly weightless titanium sets to sets so big and bulky they belong on a wagon train. Just make sure you have enough pots, cups, and spoons for everyone on the trip. Also, if you are handling hot stuff, have a plan, whether it is bringing a pot grabber, using bandannas or a chef mitt.

**Grill**: Have a grill big enough to cook your meats and other goodies for everyone in the party. Visualize how you will be using a grill. Will you be setting it up on logs? Does it have legs? I use a very small titanium grill when going solo, but a bigger one when in a group.

**Frying pan**: Frying pans can be used for more than just fish. They can be used to sauté vegetables, stir-fry rice, make quesadillas, and, of course, make breakfast. Backpacking-size aluminum frying pans with a folding handle make toting and stowing them practical for backpackers.

**Cup**: Plastic cups are lightest. Make sure they are durable enough, can be used for hot or cold drinks, and can hold adequate amounts. Insulated cups are good for winter, but in milder weather they end up keeping your coffee too hot for too long. No glass in the backcountry.

**Utensils**: The spoon is the most versatile utensil in the backcountry. It can do almost anything that a fork can, yet a fork cannot quite do what a spoon can. That must be why they invented what is known as a "spork," which looks like a spoon except it has tines on the front. Plastic ones are lightest.

I bring an ultralight one-blade knife when by myself, but a more elaborate one if in a group. Make sure your knife includes a can opener if you are toting canned goods.

Cooking in the backcountry can be challenging. However, with the right utensils and frame of mind, it can not only be fun but also enhance your backpacking experience.

# 13

## Moses Creek Backpack

### Overview

Take a gorgeous coastal overnighter to a fine campsite on tidal Moses Creek near St. Augustine. This trip first winds through well-marked oak woods to an overlook. From there, cross freshwater upper Moses Creek and then traverse partly wooded uplands to regal live oaks, ending on a hickory bluff camp with a fine view.

**Distance & Configuration**: 11.6-mile there-and-back
**Difficulty**: Easy
**Outstanding Features**: Coastal hike, great campsite, views from campsite
**Scenery**: 5
**Solitude**: 3
**Family-Friendly**: 4
**Canine-Friendly**: 5
**Fees/Permits**: No fees or permit required
**Best Season**: November through early April
**Maps**: Moses Creek Conservation Area
**For More Info**: St. Johns Water Management District, 4049 Reid St, Palatka, FL 32177, 386-329-4500, https://www.sjrwmd.com/
**Finding the Trailhead**: From exit 305 on I-95 west of Crescent Beach, take FL 206 east for 4.4 miles to the East Entrance to Moses Creek Conservation Area. Along the way you will pass the West Entrance. GPS trailhead coordinates: 29.757459, -81.275832

Moses Creek Conservation Area, managed by St. Johns Water Management District, protects one of the last undeveloped tidal creeks in the St. Johns River basin. Comprised of Moses Creek, its adjacent marshes and upland freshwater, as well as regal live oaks, laurel oaks, and fire-managed sandhill prairies, scattered with pines, fashion a charming mosaic through which to

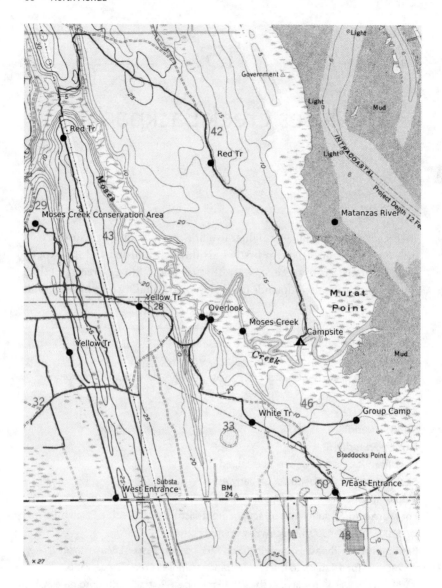

backpack to an inviting backcountry campsite on a hickory bluff overlooking Moses Creek and points beyond.

The campsite offers a picnic table, fire ring, benches, and tent sites. It's a great place to be. The downside? You have to bring your own drinking water, as Moses Creek at the campsite is brackish. You will cross a freshwater section of Moses Creek a few miles in if you want to get it and treat it from there. I've just toted mine from the trailhead. The campsite is first-come,

Author overlooks tidal Moses Creek.

first-served, dominated by hickory trees and complemented with palms and oaks. The camp faces south, catching the breeze during warm conditions, and is somewhat sheltered from the cooler north winds. A trail leads down the bluff to Moses Creek.

The trails to the campsite are double-track, well-marked and -maintained. The hike is a breeze, though you do have to tackle some sandy segments. Leave the East Entrance of the area on the White Trail under tall pines with an understory of scrub oaks and palmetto. Soon pass the first of several mountain biker–only trails (not shown on map). At 0.3 mile, the White Trail splits left, intersecting the first of several unblazed side roads. Stay with the blazes. Ahead, pass a spur to the group campsite and keep straight. Cross a sandy section of trail and then merge into oak-dominated woods.

At 1.2 miles, meet the Yellow Trail. For now, stay right with the White Trail, heading 0.2 mile to a boat launch/landing on Moses Creek and a bluff with a fine view into and across the estuarine marsh, where you will be later. Backtrack and join the Yellow Trail, dipping to bridge a fresh tributary of Moses Creek and then opening onto a big power line. Continue under the power line just a bit and meet the Red Trail, running under a lesser transmission line, at 2.3 miles. This is the least appealing part of the hike as you trudge the sand north. Bridge the freshwater segment of Moses Creek at 3.3 miles; then continue north, curving right into woods.

The Red Trail runs along a small hill above a tributary of Moses Creek, then reaches the north property boundary at 3.8 miles. Turn east along a fence line, then soon turn south, running along the edge of palmetto prairie to your right and scrubby woods to your left. The crown of a hill here is perceptible in the distance. Keep southeast and enter regal live oaks at 5.2 miles. Pop out along Moses Creek and then turn right, climbing to the hickory bluff campsite at 6.0 miles. Such a beautiful, valuable piece of land, here for you to backpack camp on free of charge. Enjoy the view of Moses Creek in the near, the Matanzas River in the yon, and populated Anastasia Island facing the Atlantic Ocean.

## Mileages

0.0 East entrance
1.2 0.2-mile spur to view/boat access
3.3 Bridge freshwater segment of Moses Creek
5.2 Enter live oaks
6.0 Campsite, backtrack
11.6 East entrance

# 14

## Rice Creek Sanctuary

### Overview

This one-night adventure takes you not only to a cool camping area with a trail shelter but also through gorgeous Rice Creek Swamp—the dry-footed way—using old rice plantation levees and the astonishing 1,886-foot Hoffman Crossing boardwalk.

---

**Distance & Configuration**: 8.8-mile loop with spurs on each end
**Difficulty**: Easy-moderate
**Outstanding Features**: Gorgeous swamp hardwood forest, Hoffman Crossing boardwalk
**Scenery**: 5
**Solitude**: 3
**Family-Friendly**: 2
**Canine-Friendly**: 1
**Fees/Permits**: No fees or permits required
**Best Season**: Mid-November through March
**Maps**: Rice Creek Conservation Area
**For More Info**: St. Johns Water Management District, 4049 Reid St, Palatka, FL 32177, 386-329-4500, https://www.sjrwmd.com/
**Finding the Trailhead**: From the intersection of FL 19 and FL 100 on the west side of Palatka, take FL 100 west for 4.3 miles to the trailhead entrance on your left. GPS trailhead coordinates: 29.683166, -81.732830

---

Rice Creek Sanctuary is one of the most memorable spots of my Florida Trail thru-hike. The heart of the swamp truly deserves the moniker *sanctuary*. As Florida backpackers know, swamps are beautiful but can be challenging wet slogs. However, at Rice Creek you can explore this gorgeous wooded wetland while walking on two centuries–old levees built when this was a rice plantation. Innumerable bridges link the levees where gaps

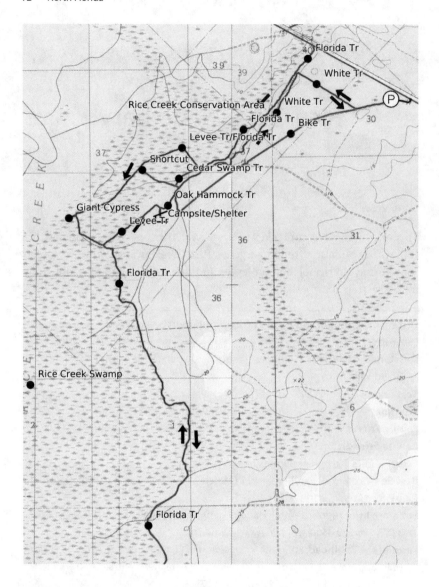

exist. After trekking the levees, you get a second treat—Hoffman Crossing, a bridged crossing of Rice Creek Swamp.

The camping here is fine, too. Overnight at a designated site that includes not only tent sites, fire ring, and pump well under live oaks but also a two-story, screened-in trail shelter dubbed the "Rice Creek Hilton."

The backpack begins innocuously, leaving the trailhead on a gated sand road dubbed the Bike Trail. The elevated double-track heads southwest;

This backpack is known for its extensive swamp boardwalks.

then, at 0.2 mile, split right onto the grassy White Trail, westbound. At 0.7 mile, the White Trail splits left and is your return route, but you keep right on a short blue-blazed trail to quickly meet the Florida Trail. Here, head left, southbound, heading southwest, now in a magnificent swamp hammock forest of live oak draped in resurrection ferns, palm, Atlantic white cedar, red maple, and magnolia. At 0.9 mile, reach the first of countless boardwalk bridges spanning wet areas, small streams, and ecologically sensitive areas.

At 1.6 miles, the Cedar Swamp Trail leaves left. We stay right on the Florida Trail, also known here as the Levee Trail, and it joins an earthen levee built when this swamp was cleared and managed as a rice plantation. Now, the swamp is populated with cypress, gum, hornbeam, and cedar trees. The levees originally helped manage the raising and lowering of water to grow rice. The gaps in the levees are now spanned with impressive trail bridges built by the Florida Trail Association that add to the fun. Use caution on the bridges and don't cause them undue stress. They are challenging to build and maintain.

Look down at the water while on a bridge. See it flowing through the swamp? Some of the largest bridges have the deepest channels. At 1.8 miles, the trail turns southwest. At 2.1 miles, reach a shortcut heading left. Continue southwest on the Levee/Florida Trail. At 2.6 miles, a spur boardwalk leads left to an overlook of purportedly the seventh-largest cypress in the state. Curve southeast and reach an intersection at 2.9 miles. For now, turn right, staying with the Florida Trail (hide your pack if you don't want to carry it on the out-and-back). Stay with the blazes of the Florida Trail as it traces grassy roadbeds. Reenter swamp hardwoods, back on single-track trail, and then reach signed Hoffmans Crossing at 4.2 miles. Begin the fabulous segment of boardwalk bridges with handrails coursing through the heart of Rice Creek Swamp. Soak in the beauty of this wild wetland for 1,886 feet and then emerge back onto grassy double-track at 4.6 miles.

Now, you get to backtrack Hoffmans Crossing, then return to join the Levee Trail at 6.3 miles. Head northeasterly back on a levee for 0.4 mile; then split right on the Oak Hammock Trail, bridge a canal, and reach the short spur to the Rice Creek Hilton shelter and campsite at 6.8 miles. Fire ring, benches, a pump well, picnic table, and tent sites are next to the two-story shelter with a lower screened-in resting area and second-floor sleeping area accessible by ladder.

After leaving the shelter, continue 7.0 miles to an intersection, where a spur leads right to the Bike Trail. If you want to stay high and dry, take the Bike Trail 1.6 miles back to the trailhead. If you desire a little more wet wandering, take the White Trail northeast, passing a spur to the Levee Trail shortcut. The White Trail works the margin between pine woods to the right and lush hammock forest to the left. Be warned, it is usually wet. At 8.1 miles, the White Trail turns right and you have completed the loop. Make a 0.7 mile backtrack to the trailhead, completing the Rice Creek Sanctuary backpack.

## Mileages

0.0   Parking area
0.7   Join Florida Trail
2.9   Leave levees
4.2   Begin Hoffmans Crossing
4.6   Backtrack
6.8   Rice Creek Hilton shelter
8.8   Parking area

### About Outdoor Sleeping Arrangements

One winter night I was backpacking the Florida Trail in the Apalachicola National Forest. A front had gone through, and the temperatures were dropping, so I decided not to set up my tent, since subfreezing temperatures would prohibit mosquitoes.

While lying in the open, under star-filled clear skies, snug in my bag, the wind began to blow, increasing so fiercely I could feel it push into my sleeping bag. I began to chill, then get colder and colder, until by dawn it seemed as if I was sleeping in the open without a bag. What a long night.

Having the proper sleeping bag can mean the difference between a good night's rest and a miserable night followed by an exhausted next day. The primary concerns for backpackers when choosing a sleeping bag are warmth, space, and weight. Match your sleeping bag to the season and situation. For example, use a fairly warm sleeping bag in North Florida in January. If you are trekking along at Jonathan Dickinson State Park in April, choose the lightest bag possible.

During the Florida backpacking season, in all but the warmest times I recommend a sleeping bag comfort rated from 40°. These bags can handle cold fronts in winter and cool spring nights, without weighing too much. If the temperature dips, just put on more clothes and you'll be fine. In warmer conditions use a simple zippered fleece blanket—one item you can get cheaply.

When going on one-night trips, backpackers can worry less about weight and space of the sleeping bag, and you can choose the exact temperature bag to suit that night's needs. Generally speaking, today's modern down-filled sleeping bags can compress to small sizes, so space is less of an issue than ever.

For additional comfort, consider carrying a small camp pillow or bundle your clothes up under your head. Don't underestimate the importance of a pillow.

Sleeping pads are every bit as critical to a good night's rest as is a sleeping bag. In cold conditions while backpacking, I combine a simple closed-cell foam pad, 6 feet in length, with a lightweight, three-quarter-length 48-inch self-inflating air mattress on top of it. The lighter-model air mattresses come in under a pound each; they are the most popular today and are usually used as stand-alone mattresses for weight-conscious backpackers.

A closed-cell foam pad be used not only under you while sleeping but also around the campsite and will prevent popping a hole in your air mattress should you use it sitting around camp or by the fire. The foam pad eases things while you're leaning against an oak log or sitting on wet ground. By the way, a thin ground sheet cut a little larger than the size of your sleeping pad or tent helps keep you and your stuff dry from ground moisture.

Remember that proper sleeping arrangements can enhance your backpacking experience.

# *Central Florida*

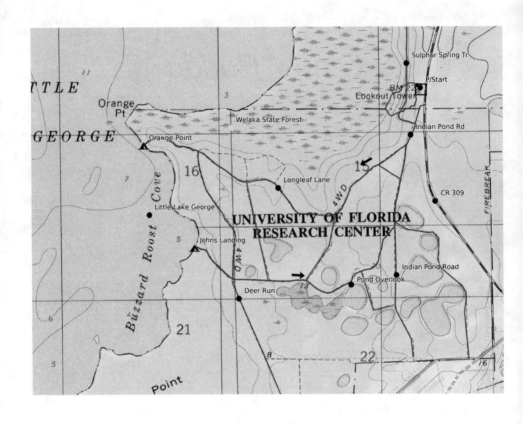

# 15

## Welaka State Forest Backpack

### Overview

This overnighter is as much about the camping as the trail trekking and is perfect for a break-in one-night backpack. Follow a series of easy grassy tracks through pine and oak forests to a pair of gorgeous shoreline campsites set in live oak hammocks overlooking big and wild Little Lake George. Your return route leads through the state forest back to the trailhead.

**Distance & Configuration**: 4.1-mile balloon loop
**Difficulty**: Easy
**Outstanding Features**: Little Lake George, excellent campsites
**Scenery**: 5
**Solitude**: 3
**Family-Friendly**: 5
**Canine-Friendly**: 5
**Fees/Permits**: Fee-based camping permit required
**Best Season**: November through mid-May
**Maps**: Welaka State Forest Map
**For More Info**: Welaka State Forest, PO Box 174, Welaka, FL 32193-0174, 386-292-2478, https://www.fdacs.gov/; Campsite reservations: 877-879-3859, https://www.reserveamerica.com/
**Finding the Trailhead**: From downtown Palatka, take US 17 south across the St. Johns River and stay with it for 11.7 miles. Then turn right onto CR 309 and follow it for 7.8 miles to the signed Johns Landing trailhead on your right. GPS trailhead coordinates: 29.453350, -81.657308

Welaka State Forest is set on the shores of not-so-little Little Lake George, essentially a wide section of the St. Johns River. A network of wide double-track trails lead through the 2,300-acre reserve, first set aside in 1935 as a federal Depression-era works project fish hatchery, ultimately to be handed over to the Florida Forest Service in 1992.

Wide sand trails traverse Welaka State Forest.

Now managed for timber, natural features, and wildlife, the state forest boasts more than 4 miles of frontage on Little Lake George. Across the lake lies the vast Ocala National Forest, fashioning a remote and wild setting for backpackers who overnight at one of the two backcountry campsites on the dark-sky shoreline. These fee-based campsites must be reserved in advance, but when you get the campsite, it is yours alone. And they are superlative camps, ideal for one-night trips. As its name implies, Orange Point is set on a peninsula jutting into Lake George, shaded by regal live oaks complemented with palms. Johns Landing, regarded as the better of the two camps, is situated in a cove overlooking wide waters and is also shaded by live oaks. Both have picnic tables, fire rings, and lake access. Water can be had from Little Lake George.

Some may think the double-track trails less exciting, but they have the advantage of allowing you to soak in the trailside scenery rather than watching every footfall. But to that end, a hiker-only single-track St. Johns Trail (not shown on map) does roughly parallel the loop recommended here. However, the hiker-only trail is often overgrown and wet, whereas the double-tracks are easy on the feet and eyes.

Either way, you will find the campsites an ample reward, perfect for families or a good place to initiate backpackers seeking a guaranteed-quality campsite. The trail system is well signed, blazed, and maintained. The trek starts off on CR 309 at the Johns Landing trailhead and offers a restroom and shaded picnic tables. From there, join the single-track Forest Education Trail, leaving near the still-standing fire tower at the trailhead. Enter mixed forest of pine, palmetto, and oak. At 0.1 mile, open onto a double-track and kiosk. Here, head left on the St. Johns Landing Trail, a wide path as it curves east to reach a gate and Indian Pond Road at 0.2 mile (closed to public vehicles). Split right and follow Indian Pond Road for 0.1 mile; then split right with Longleaf Lane for Orange Point Campsite. Now, travel west in pine/palmetto woods mixed with live oak domes.

The walking is easy. Parts of the trail are open overhead, necessitating a hat. At 1.0 mile, bridge a small creek by culvert. At 1.3 miles, reach an intersection. Stay straight with the 0.3-mile spur to Orange Point, delving into a live oak hammock where you find the shoreline campsite lying under live oaks. This beautiful camp is a little more protected from winds coming off Lake George than is the St. Johns Landing Campsite.

After backtracking from the campsite, head south on double-track Deer Run, cruising mixed woods. At 2.3 miles, split right on Hammock Hideaway, heading for the lake. At 2.5 miles, come to Johns Landing Campsite, a true hammock hideaway, set under moss-draped live oaks, pines, and palmettos, along with palms aplenty. Little Lake George extends to the distant shore.

Your return route heads east from the shore, staying with Hammock Hideaway, a narrower double-track atop an elevated berm above sometimes-wet woods with bay trees. At 3.2 miles, pass a pond overlook, where you can gain a view of a grassy tarn bordered in low live oaks, adding biodiversity to the experience. Curve north, entering a live oak grove and then meeting Indian Pond Road at 3.5 miles. Head left here, northbound, passing more ponds. At 3.8 miles, complete the loop portion of the hike, backtracking 0.3 mile to complete the backpack.

## Mileages

0.0   Johns Landing trailhead
1.6   Orange Point Campsite
2.5   Johns Landing Campsite
4.1   Johns Landing trailhead

# 16

## Holly Hammock Backpack

### Overview

This excellent short overnighter takes place at Ross Prairie State Forest. Start the backpack alternating between deep hardwood hammock and open turkey oak/pine stands before visiting a grassy wetland pond. Make a wide circuit around the pond to reach a secluded backcountry campsite amid oaks. From there, circle through mixed woods before returning to the trailhead.

---

**Distance & Configuration**: 3.1-mile balloon loop

**Difficulty**: Easy

**Outstanding Features**: Varied ecosystems, good family backpack

**Scenery**: 3

**Solitude**: 3

**Family-Friendly**: 5

**Canine-Friendly**: 5

**Fees/Permits**: Camping fee and daily permit required

**Best Season**: Mid-October through April

**Maps**: Ross Prairie State Forest

**For More Info**: Ross Prairie State Forest, Indian Lake Forestry Station, 6675 NE 40 Avenue Road, Ocala, FL 34479; 352-732-1779, Campsite reservations: https://www.reserveamerica.com/, 877-879-3859

**Finding the Trailhead**: From exit 350 on I-75 near Ocala, take FL 200 south for 10.8 miles to the Ross State Forest entrance on your left. Join a paved road and immediately park on your right at the designated overnight primitive campsite parking. Do not park at the day-use area near the campground. GPS trailhead coordinates: 29.036877, -82.299841

---

Ross Prairie State Forest, more than 3,500 acres in size, is a relatively new parcel in the Florida State Forest system. The Holly Hammock Trail is your backpacking conduit, a perfect easy backpack for families or just someone who wants a little overnight respite in nature. The fee-based campsite must

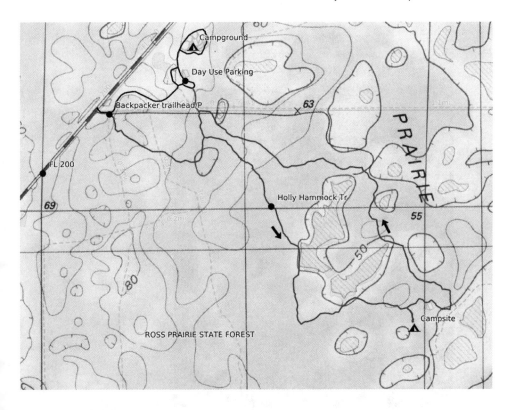

be reserved ahead of time. The camp is set in an oak forest with fire ring and picnic table. Bring your own water, which is not a problem since the hike to the campsite is short. Remember, do not park in the day-use area. Use the designated primitive campsite parking area only.

From the primitive campsite parking area, cross a sand fire lane and then pick up a single-track path in rolling pine/turkey oaks and wiregrass woods. Cross another fire lane; then dip into rich hammock woods, with tall, moss-draped oaks. One evergreen you will see is the trail's namesake, American holly. The prickly-leafed tree with the pale mottled trunk is scattered throughout the hammock understory. Some of these hollies are positively huge—for holly trees. The evergreens can be found the length of the Panhandle and down the inland Florida peninsula to lower Central Florida.

At 0.4 mile, reach an intersection. Head right, now on the Holly Hammock Trail. At 0.6 mile, rise to more open forest of turkey oak, longleaf pine, and tan wiregrass. Top over the hillock and return to denser woods dominated by live oaks. At 0.8 mile, the loop climbs to an artificial sand berm ringing a grassy seasonal wetland. Walk the white sand berm and then quickly drop off it at 0.6 mile, wandering among the reddish trunks of

Warmly clad backpacker heads for the campsite.

sparkleberry bushes, wild azalea, and laurel oaks. The trail briefly rejoins the berm. Ramble through flatwoods, and, at 1.3 miles, meet the spur trail leading right to the loop's backcountry campsite. The simple camp, shaded in oaks, offers a picnic table and fire ring—and a spot for your tent. Remember to bring your own water.

Back on the main loop at 1.6 miles, come alongside the edge of a sizeable tawny prairie. Soak in this evergreen-ringed wetland before turning back toward the trailhead. At 1.9 miles, come yet again to the berm surrounding the grassy wetland. And again the trail quickly turns away from it. Hike through a mix of forest from sand pines to live oaks. Blazes keep you apprised of your whereabouts. At 2.6 miles, split left on a sand road. Shortly reach the single-track trail connecting the Holly Hammock Trail to the day-use area. Head left, away from the sand road on the single-track path, to complete the loop at 2.7 miles. From here, backtrack on the primitive campground access spur, finishing the rewarding backpack at 3.1 miles.

## Mileages

0.0   Primitive camp parking area
0.4   Join Holly Hammock Trail
1.3   Backcountry campsite
3.1   Primitive camp parking area

## Light Options for the Long Nights of Winter

A friend and I were backpacking Torreya State Park. At noon, a low December sun stretched overhead, then fell to the west, elongating the shadows of leafless, skeletal trees. A creeping chill pushed into our campsite with the darkening dusk.

It wasn't even six o'clock. But it was time to light our campsite.

Winter is the prime season for Florida backpackers, despite the short days and long nights, when fall's golden light turns to winter's pale, weak rays that don't even stick around that long. In Clermont, roughly the geographic center of the Florida peninsula, the hours of daylight reach a low of 10 hours 19 minutes of light per day. That leaves 12-plus hours of darkness. And for the backpacker, that can be a long time.

However, backpackers have an array of light options, from old-fashioned candles to ultralight headlamps. Depending on the situation, I use them all to illuminate the night, not only to help stay awake but also to gather wood, cook dinner, slip into the sleeping bag, and keep from stumbling around the campsite.

Candles still have their place. They give a soft light, perfect for general illumination. A little foil will enhance a candle's brightness and also block a breeze that makes them burn fast or blow out. An upside: candle wax dripped onto kindling makes for a good emergency fire starter. A downside: their susceptibility to wind—also you simply can't carry them around. Small, battery-operated lanterns are yet another option. They use 2–3 small batteries and provide decent illumination.

Headlamps are the best all-around backpacking light. Here, a battery-operated light is connected to a strap fitting around your head. The headlamp is hands-free, and the beam shines wherever the user is looking. These generally operate on three AAA batteries, leaving them lightweight. Variations of this include small lights powered by nickel-sized watch batteries that clip onto the bill of a ball cap. Headlamps are best for backpackers because they weigh so little. Check your batteries before embarking on your backpack!

Lightweight, plastic solar-charged lights, such as those by Luci, are inexpensive, weigh mere ounces, yet can spread a soft light onto a campsite when hung from a nearby tree or line, for stumble-free camping. I highly recommend them for backpackers. These are slower recharging in winter, so have it fully charged before departing, and don't expect much recharging during your trip.

What about a hand-held flashlight? They are still used by a few backpackers and still have their place, mostly as a backup for the other light options during the long nights of winter.

# 17

## Ocklawaha Prairie Backpack

### Overview

This one-night overnight adventure features a fine backcountry campsite on a short trek with plenty of highlights to see along the way. St. Johns Water Management District manages the land, formerly part of the ill-fated Cross Florida Barge Canal. The backpack first stops by a prairie wildlife observation deck and then moves through rich woodlands to reach a fine live oak hammock campsite situated alongside the now-canalized Ocklawaha River.

**Distance & Configuration**: 5.0-mile balloon loop
**Difficulty**: Easy
**Outstanding Features**: Wildlife observation tower, good campsite
**Scenery**: 4
**Solitude**: 4
**Family-Friendly**: 5
**Canine-Friendly**: 5
**Fees/Permits**: No fees or permits required
**Best Season**: November through mid-April
**Maps**: Ocklawaha Prairie Restoration Area
**For More Info**: St. Johns Water Management District, 4049 Reid St, Palatka, FL 32177, 386-329-4500, https://www.sjrwmd.com/
**Finding the Trailhead**: From the intersection of FL 35 and FL 40 in Silver Springs, take FL 40 east for 10.8 miles to CR 314A. Turn right and take CR 314A south for 6.5 miles to 137th Ave, Old River Road (this right turn comes as CR 314A is curving left). Turn right on 137th Ave and follow it 0.7 miles to the Ocklawaha Prairie Restoration Area trailhead on your left. The sand road quickly dead-ends in an open field. GPS trailhead coordinates: 29.107041, -81.905004

This 6,077-acre Ocklawaha Prairie Restoration Area, east of Ocala, is part of the ongoing restoration of the Ocklawaha River basin after it was altered in preparation for the river's incorporation into the Cross Florida Barge

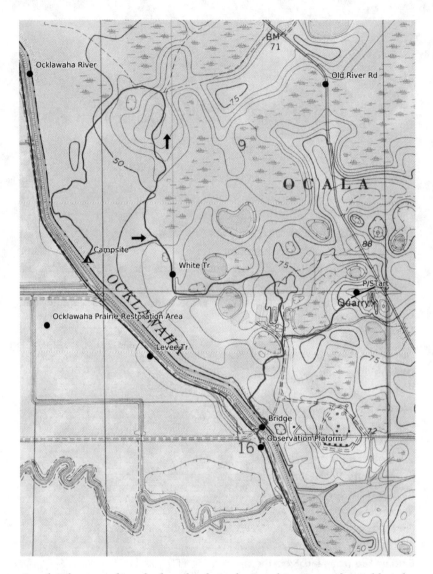

Canal. Like most disturbed wetlands in the Sunshine State, the Ocklawaha will never be the same as it was in a pristine condition, but at least the state restored the floodplain, thus enhancing native plant and animal life.

Backpackers will enjoy the easy, well-marked, well-maintained and well-blazed path system, mostly double-track trails. The first-come, first-served campsite is set under massive live oaks shading a grassy understory, next to the canalized Ocklawaha. The camp presents a picnic table, fire ring, and hand pump well with sulfurous water. When camping here I've just used the nearby Ocklawaha water. Tent sites are ample.

This campsite is set in a picturesque live oak hammock.

Join the grassy, blazed White Trail heading downhill in a mix of fields and woods, westbound. At 0.3 mile, in an open, grassy intersection with a concrete building foundation nearby, the loop part of the White Trail leaves right. Here, stay left toward the prairie observation platform. Trace the blazes as the path flits off and on old roads. Cruise through bottomland woods, meadows, and live oaks. Emerge onto a road near private property at 0.8 mile. Here, turn right on the road, immediately bridging a canal that currently carries the balance of the Ocklawaha River flow, going by the name of C 212. That moniker just doesn't have the zing that "Ocklawaha" has rolling off your tongue.

Once across C 212, you are on the Levee Trail. It makes a 10.8-mile loop around the whole Ocklawaha marsh and is a good bicycle ride, especially for bicycling birders. The marsh is rich with avian life, from ducks to songbirds to raptors. Once on the Levee Trail, go left to the wooden observation deck and overlook the marsh prairie. Your wildlife experience will depend on time of year, but expect birdsong to serenade you.

Backtrack from the observation deck almost back to the trailhead, then, at 1.3 miles, take the unwalked part of the White Trail as it heads north across grassy lands mixed with trees islands. Watch for sandhill cranes in this area. At 1.6 miles, the trail turns west and borders the Ocala National Forest, traveling in scrub oaks and pines along the national forest/restoration area boundary. The plentiful deer of the locale know no boundaries. Stay with the white blazes as the trail jumps off and on old roadbeds. At 2.1 miles, reach the loop portion of the backpack.

Stay right, northbound, in sand pine scrub. Quickly dip through a swamp strand. Roll in hills. At 2.8 miles, the White Trail opens into pine/palmetto woods as it turns south.

At 3.3 miles, the White Trail comes alongside canal C 212. Oaks and palms are rife here. Roughly parallel the canal and at 3.6 miles come to the designated backcountry campsite under alluring mature live oaks. Plenty of level spots are available for tenters. The grassy understory beneath the live oaks reaches all the way to the canal. The White Trail turns east from the campsite, and you complete the loop portion of the hike at 3.8 miles. From there it is 1.2 miles back to the trailhead, concluding the backpack.

## Mileages

    0.0   Ocklawaha Prairie Restoration Area trailhead
    0.3   Loop portion of White Trail leaves right; go left
    0.8   Cross C 212 canal, head to observation deck
    3.6   Campsite
    5.0   Ocklawaha Prairie Restoration Area trailhead

# 18

## Ocala North Backpack

### Overview

Start this first-rate adventure at first-rate Juniper Springs Recreation Area. Join the Florida Trail to traverse the stark yet stunning Juniper Prairie Wilderness. From there, undulate through sand pine scrub and then backpack along eye-appealing Hopkins Prairie to enter vast longleaf pine forests. Stop by the fabled 88 Store, finally making your way to hike's end at Lake Ocklawaha.

**Distance & Configuration**: 39.1-mile end-to-end
**Difficulty**: Difficult due to distance
**Outstanding Features**: Juniper Prairie Wilderness, Hopkins Prairie, Lake Ocklawaha
**Scenery**: 5
**Solitude**: 3 (some sections busy)
**Family-Friendly**: 3
**Canine-Friendly**: 2
**Fees/Permits**: No fees or permits required
**Best season**: Mid-November through mid-April
**Maps**: Ocala National Forest
**For More Info**: Ocala National Forest, Seminole Ranger District, 40929 SR 19, Umatilla, FL 32784, 352-669-3153, https://www.fs.usda.gov/recarea/florida/recarea/?recid=83528
**Finding the Trailhead**: To reach the northern trailhead from Ocala, drive east on SR 40 for 12 miles to Marion CR 314. Turn left on CR 314 and follow it 18 miles to FL 19. Turn left on FL 19 and follow it north for 11.7 miles to turn left on Rodman Dam Road; follow it 3.2 miles to the dam. The parking area is the north side below the dam. To reach the backpack's beginning from Rodman Dam, backtrack to FL 19 and follow it for 28.2 miles; then turn right onto FL 40 and follow it 4.4 miles to turn right into Juniper Springs Recreation Area and its fee parking area. GPS trailhead coordinates: Rodman Dam: 29.509335, -81.803021, Juniper Springs Recreation Area: 29.181450, -81.712937

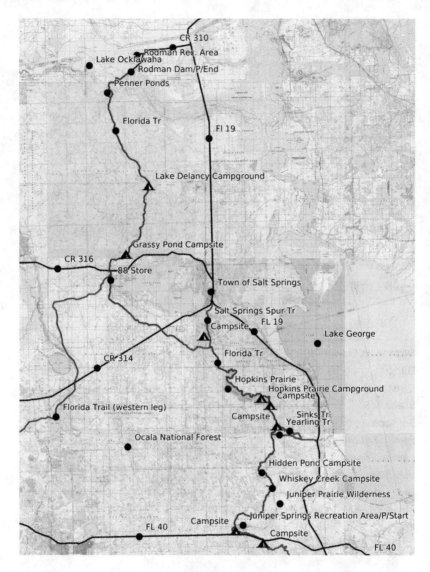

This backpack explores varied and appealing scenery and is a Florida back-packer lifetime goal. Jump straight into the hike with a trek through 14,283-acre Juniper Prairie Wilderness, where the trail weaves through low-slung pine scrub, where the sun blazes down from above, where bears roam along Whiskey Creek, where Pats Island reveals its past, and the cool waters of Hidden Pond await your arrival. The tops of hills and prairies deliver surprising views. Next comes vast Hopkins Prairie, the largest prairie in the Ocala National Forest, where you find a campground, water, and more vistas while hiking along the nexus of land and wetland.

Entering the sand pine scrub of Juniper Prairie Wilderness.

Next, backpack through rolling pine/wiregrass woodland once prevalent over much of Florida. Saunter over three "islands" in the Ocala National Forest—Kerr Island, Salt Springs Island, and Riverside Island. These islands are not surrounded by water in the traditional sense but are islands of fertile soil, supporting rich stands of longleaf and slash pine, surrounded by the more sterile soils where the sand pine scrub thrives. This final, most northerly segment of the Florida Trail in the Ocala National Forest passes Lake Delancy Campground and then the Penner Ponds, the last prairie/pond complex in the forest. Finally, reach picturesque Lake Ocklawaha, ending on the far side of Rodman Dam.

This northern section of the Florida Trail is less used than in other parts of the Ocala and thus offers more opportunities for solitude. Secure, fee parking at Rodman Recreation Area adds 1 mile to the backpack. If you are looking to shorten the adventure, consider the 25-mile trip from Juniper Springs to the 88 Store. The 10-mile trip from Juniper Springs to Hopkins Prairie is the most heavily traveled trail segment in all of the Ocala National Forest. In contrast, solitude seekers may prefer the 29-mile trail segment from Hopkins Prairie to Lake Ocklawaha.

This backpack proffers a wide variety of overnighting opportunities. You can choose from a few established backcountry campsites, find your own using leave-no-trace principles, or stay at one of two developed campgrounds along the way. You will pass several segments with limited easy water, so keep your water containers filled. Hopkins Prairie Campground has a hand pump well. Water can also be had from ponds and streams.

Notes: Numerous forest roads and fire lanes will be crossed while traversing the Ocala National Forest. However, the Florida Trail is well signed throughout the route. Though you will see a few established trailside camps, be prepared to seek out a site. A large water carrier will extend your range of campable locations. Consider caching water at forest road crossings.

Begin the adventure by leaving west from the Juniper Springs entrance road on the Florida Trail, entering the most popular section of Florida Trail in the Ocala National Forest. Pass established campsites carved from scrub woods ahead. At 1.1 miles, enter signed Juniper Prairie Wilderness. Frequent burns leave much of the sky open overhead. The trailhead is often sandy and loose from hiker traffic. You will see old jeep roads crossing the Florida Trail in places. Appreciate the repeated transitions from scrub to tall pines to grassy marshes, depending on elevation and exposure. At 3.1 miles, pass a few palms and the ephemeral outflow of a prairie to your left. Juniper Prairie stretches into the yon.

At 4.2 miles, cross small Whiskey Creek on plank footbridge. Find a decent campsite to the right of the trail after the creek crossing. Roll through hilly, sandy scrub woods, northbound, along the east flank of Juniper Prairie. At 5.4 miles, come to Hidden Pond, nestled in sand scrub hills. This is a fine swimming hole with campsites on far side of the pond. Be apprised this is the busiest backcountry campsite in the entire Ocala National Forest and is often picked clean of firewood. Continue in sandy hills dividing grassy ponds and prairies.

At 8.2 miles, intersect The Yearling Trail after climbing away from Juniper Prairie. It leads right to Pats Island and Long Cemetery, setting of the celebrated book and movie *The Yearling*. Keep straight, now in tall slash and longleaf pines mixed with oak thickets and live oak copses. At 8.8 miles, reach a campsite in tall pines. Just ahead the Sink Hole Trail leaves right. Stay straight on the Florida Trail and then cross Forest Road (FR) 46, leaving Juniper Prairie Wilderness. Keep north in live oaks, palmetto, and sand pines. At 9.9 miles, pass a small sinkhole on trail left just before crossing FR 50. Ahead, hike adjacent to a deep sink/good water source/swimming hole. A spur trail leads right to access the sink. A campsite is just ahead.

The Florida Trail begins running along the edge of Hopkins Prairie. At 10.8 miles, make the Hopkins Prairie Campground access road and alternate parking. At 11.2 miles, reach the edge of Hopkins Prairie Campground to your left, with developed campsites and pump well water. Here, the Florida

Trail turns right along prairie, enjoy scenic vistas of open water, grassy wetlands, and forest beyond. The Florida Trail often travels in the open sands and grasses on prairie edge. Campsites can be found in live oaks and tall pines. A sense of remoteness falls over the land.

At 15.8 miles, leave north from Hopkins Prairie, with campsites before and after departing the prairie. The Florida Trail heads northwest in scrub oaks, soon crossing FR 33. At 16.4 miles, cross FR 50 on a hill. Make noticeable descent, enter rolling sand pines. At 16.9 miles, pass the first of a few small depression marshes. At 17.6 miles, intersect the Salt Springs Spur Trail. Water and camping can be found on west side of ponds about a quarter mile up that trail. The Salt Springs Spur Trail leads 3 miles to Salt Springs Recreation Area, and a campground with hot showers and water. The nearby hamlet of Salt Springs has a small grocery store and eateries. Keep straight on Florida Trail, entering oak scrub with a superstory of sand pine overhead.

At 18.8 miles, cross sandy FR 58. Enter Salt Springs Island, named for being a fertile island of longleaf pine and turkey oak amid the sand scrub. Traverse hills and swales, crossing paved CR 314. Occasional oak domes break up the pines. At 22.0 miles, leave Salt Springs Island, reentering sand pine scrub. At 23.8 miles, enter Kerr Island after crossing FR 63. You are back in pine/turkey oak/wiregrass. The Florida Trail soon curves north, entering a hilly area near residences with lots of jeep trails. At 24.9 miles, find the short jeep trail right to the iconic 88 Store, the bar/store with hiker register. They are very laissez-faire and may be offering showers and laundry, and even hiker shuttles. They have a front porch, beer, drinks, ice cream, snacks, pool, darts, and a place to plug in your phone.

At 25.2 miles, the western leg of Florida Trail merges from your left. Ahead, cross CR 316, then leave Kerr Island for good. Enter sand pine scrub, eastbound to cross FR 11 at 26.1 miles. At 27.0 miles, a signed spur leads left to all-wheel-drive auto-accessible Grassy Pond. Camping is in a woods-bordered grass field. Wade into Grassy Pond for water.

At 30.7 miles, visit a dry sink with live oaks, laurel oaks, and palms. Another sink lies ahead. At 31.3 miles, come beside large Delancy West OHV Campground, with water from Lake Delancy. Ahead, cross FR 66, keep north in the gorgeous, pine/live oak/wiregrass forest of Riverside Island. At 33.6 miles, descend alongside a sink filled with large live oaks and then cross sandy FR 11. Oaks become more prevalent the closer you get to Lake Ocklawaha.

At 36.7 miles, cross FR 74. Ahead, the sometimes-faint blue-blazed spur trail leads left around Penner Ponds with a campsite and difficult water from Penner Ponds. The Florida Trail keeps straight in live oaks then mixed woods. At 37.6 miles, intersect the faint north end of Penner Ponds spur. The Florida Trail leaves the ponds northeast for Lake Ocklawaha. At 38.1 miles, reach the shores of Lake Ocklawaha in gorgeous moss-draped live oaks with campsites. Head right along shore to reach Rodman Dam and FR 11. Head left across the dam, savoring big lake views. At 39.1 miles, reach the parking area just beyond Rodman Dam spillway and backpack's end. Fee parking at Rodman Recreation Area is a mile farther on.

## Mileages

|      |                                                      |
|------|------------------------------------------------------|
| 0.0  | Juniper Springs Recreation Area                      |
| 1.1  | Juniper Prairie Wilderness                           |
| 4.2  | Whiskey Creek, campsite                              |
| 5.4  | Hidden Pond, campsites                               |
| 8.2  | The Yearling Trail leaves right                      |
| 8.8  | Campsite, Sinkhole Trail leaves right, FR 46 ahead   |
| 9.9  | FR 50, deep, small pond, campsite                   |
| 10.8 | Hopkins Prairie Campground access road, alternate parking |
| 11.2 | Hopkins Prairie Campground                           |
| 15.8 | Leave Hopkins Prairie, campsites                     |
| 16.4 | FR 90                                                |
| 17.6 | Salt Springs Spur Trail leaves right                 |
| 18.8 | Salt Springs Island                                  |
| 20.1 | Cross paved FR 11                                    |
| 20.5 | Cross paved CR 314                                   |
| 22.0 | Cross sand FR 50, leave Salt Springs Island          |
| 23.8 | Kerr Island                                          |
| 24.9 | 88 Store                                             |
| 25.2 | Intersect western leg of Florida Trail, cross CR 316 |
| 26.1 | FR 11                                                |
| 27.0 | Grassy Pond, campsites                               |
| 31.3 | Delancy West OHV Campground                          |
| 33.6 | Cross FR 11                                          |
| 36.7 | Cross FR 74, Penner Ponds                            |
| 38.1 | Lake Ocklawaha, campsites                            |
| 38.3 | FR 11, left on Rodman Dam                            |
| 39.1 | Dam spillway parking area, end of backpack           |

## Backpacker Philosophies Differ

Backpacking enthusiasts run the gamut in their methodology. On one end are the so-called backpacking purists. They generally have the best gear and are always on the lookout for the latest in high-tech offerings by the outdoor outfitting industry. And they are willing to pay for it.

Their fare usually consists of fancy freeze-dried food. Gore-Tex fabric and name-brand labels are prominently displayed on their clothing. They have the latest phone loaded with outdoor-related apps. Always prepared and ready to help the ill-prepared, they rarely get in over their heads, saving taxpayer dollars and ranger headaches by never needing to be rescued.

At the other end of the spectrum is the make-do backpacker. He or she probably borrowed half the equipment on their back and will not hesitate to tote a cast-iron skillet to fry some bacon at the campsite. They can be spotted on the trail invariably wearing too-tight jeans and combat boots. They would not be caught dead using their phone to figure out where they are.

At camp, make-do hikers try to think of ways to use the big knife in the leather case attached to their belt. An oversized cheap tent invariably pops up wherever they are. They are learning, and some will eventually move across and find their own place on the spectrum.

Two other subcategories exist: the minimalists and the gearheads. Minimalists become overly obsessed with weight, paring their gear down to such a degree that much enjoyment is lost from their wilderness experience, which has become a sheer survival test.

I once stayed with some women at a backcountry shelter who drank hot water for breakfast; they felt the weight of coffee did not justify its extravagance. Others become so concerned with pack weight they will cut off the ends of their toothbrush to save one-tenth of an ounce. However, when they tell around the campfire about how much weight they've saved, they are in hog heaven!

The gearhead has it all, literally, and it is in his pack. Around the fire, you grumble about losing a tiny screw from your fishing reel, and ten minutes later he proudly returns with the exact size screw you needed. It is a good thing he has a hot water bottle because he is going to need it to soothe those back muscles that are cramping from carrying all that extra equipment on his back.

Pack weight has always been the source of spirited backpacker discussions. As a general guide, backpackers should carry no more than 15 percent of their body weight, striving toward 10 percent. Nevertheless, wilderness adventuring has no commandments. Each person literally carries his or her own weight—and lives with their choices.

While out there, I relish the opportunities to see how others conduct business on the trails. With an open mind, I usually learn something, even if it is what not to do. To think that my way is the only way merely restricts my growth as a backpacker.

So the next time you see somebody backpacking down the trail, they are not merely putting one foot in front of the other. There is likely a philosophy in there somewhere.

# 19

## Ocala South Backpack

### Overview

This backpack traverses the south half of famed Ocala National Forest, a land of vast sand pine scrub, distant prairies, intimate ponds, and a regal stretch of the Florida Trail. Leave Clearwater Lake, working north through a mosaic of environments—hills and ponds, streams and prairies with an abundance of potential campsites from which to choose, ending this aggressive 2-night trip at pretty Juniper Springs Recreation Area.

---

**Distance & Configuration**: 28.0 miles end-to-end

**Difficulty**: Moderate-difficult

**Outstanding Features**: Farles Prairie, ponds, good campsites

**Scenery**: 5

**Solitude**: 3

**Family-Friendly**: 3

**Canine-Friendly**: 3

**Fees/Permits**: No fees or permits required

**Best Season**: Mid-November through mid-April

**Maps**: Ocala National Forest

**For more info**: Ocala National Forest, Seminole Ranger District, 40929 SR 19, Umatilla, FL 32784, 352-669-3153, https://www.fs.usda.gov/recarea/florida/recarea/?recid=83528

**Finding the Trailhead**: To reach Juniper Springs Recreation Area from exit 352 on I-75 west of Ocala, take FL 40 east for 30.5 miles to turn left into Juniper Spring Recreation Area, with overnight fee parking. To get to the backpack's beginning from Juniper Spring, continue on FL 40 east for 4.4 miles to turn right onto FL 19 south. Follow it for 14.5 miles to turn left onto CR 42, following it 6.5 miles to turn left into Clearwater Lake Recreation Area. The trailhead parking is ahead on your right: Juniper Springs Campground: 29.181369, -81.712961, Clearwater Lake Recreation Area: 28.976691, -81.550314

---

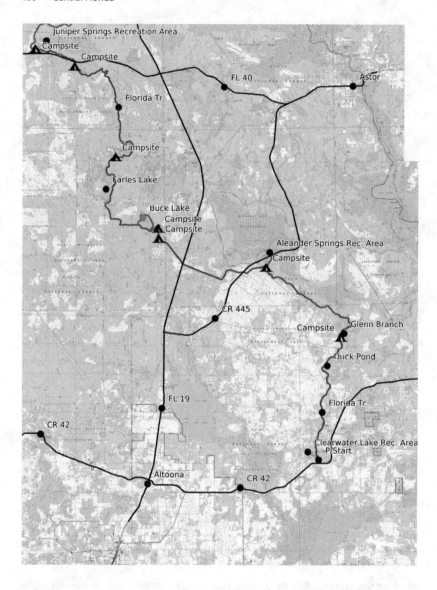

This popular backpack is deservedly a Sunshine State classic. After all, it encompasses the first segment of the Florida Trail ever laid out, back in 1966, by Florida Trail pioneer Jim Kern. Literally, the spot where this hike starts—Clearwater Lake—is where the Florida Trail made its modest beginning. It is still a good place to start, to enjoy a menagerie of natural Florida scenes—from seepage slopes to streamside hammocks, to sand pine scrub, to live oak–bordered ponds, to open prairie. Camping possibilities vary

Overlooking ponds on Farles Prairie.

wildly along the way. You can find your own spot in the backcountry, use previously established sites (not that many of them since established camps in fire-managed woods get obscured by prescribed burns) or stay at developed campgrounds. Most campsites are found near water sources. Water can also be had from natural lakes, surface streams, and ponds, as well as developed campgrounds. Some of the ponds are quite grassy, and you have to wade into them to reach the aqua.

Other notes: Along the way you will cross many obscure forest roads and sand tracks. The major forest road crossings are noted in the narrative below and are signed at the crossings. Remember, campsites are not going to jump out at you. Long-term established sites are few. Be prepared to seek out a site. A large water carrier will extend your range of campable locations. Consider caching water at forest road crossings.

Here's a synopsis: Beginning at Clearwater Lake you can walk the first miles of the Florida Trail, laid out here in 1966. Roll through tall pines, cross one of the Ocala National Forest's few surface streams, and take a boardwalk through junglesque woods. Come near developed Alexander Springs Recreation Area. Enter the often-hilly classic sand pine scrub for which the national forest is known. Then you reach vast and beautiful Farles Prairie, the first of several scenic wetlands along which the hike passes. Live oaks and longleaf pine thrive along these waters. These prairies, collectively known as Ocala Pond, are very shallow. Vistas stretch far in this Florida prairie land. After crossing FL 40, reach Juniper Springs Recreation Area, with potable water, a campground with hot showers, and camp store with limited supplies.

Start the backpack by joining the Florida Trail northbound, sharing the trailhead with the Paisley Bicycle Trail (not shown on map). Roll through longleaf pine/wiregrass, along with a few oaks. At 2.2 miles, pass an 1800s gravesite on trail left. At 2.8 miles, cross FR 69, then descend and roll through open longleaf and scrub oak woods on a sand and pine needle footbed. Watch for trailside cacti. At 3.7 miles, skirt the west side of Duck Pond and its attendant prairie. Continue north. At 4.8 miles, pass under a major power line. Descend to a moister area and Glenn Branch at 5.3 miles, a cool, clear stream shaded by moisture-loving trees such as maple. Campsites can be found on the right before you reach the small bridged stream. Ahead, at 6.0 miles, cut through a wooded swamp on a long boardwalk, under palms, live oaks, cypress, and bay trees to cross Forest Road (FR) 539 at 6.7 miles. Here, the Florida Trail curves northwest, paralleling Alexander Springs Creek down a slope to your right.

At 8.4 miles, hike under a transmission line and enter taller woods with potential campsites. At 9.7 miles, cross a long boardwalk atop a seepage slope. At 10.1 miles, the spur trail to Alexander Springs Recreation Area leads right to potable water, developed campsites, showers, and alternate parking. Primitive campsites can be found around the trail intersection. Beyond here, the Florida Trail turns west to cross FR 69 at 10.4 miles; it then enters longleaf pine/wiregrass ecosystem.

At 11.1 miles, cross paved CR 445, staying in hilly terrain through mixed woods. At 13.5 miles, cross paved FL 19 to reach national forest trail parking. The Florida Trail angles northwest in oak scrub, skirting a trailside sinkhole before crossing sandy FR 57, aka Railroad Grade Road, at 14.4 miles. Ahead, come to good campsites at the unreliable Summit Pond (consider caching water on FR 57 if camping here). Enter a wetter area ahead, reaching Dora's Pond at 15.1 miles, with potential campsites. Hills rise from the pond. At 15.8 miles, intersect the blue-blazed Buck Lake Loop Trail. Stay left with the Florida Trail, skirting Buck Lake, and enter low-arching live oaks draped in Spanish moss.

At 16.4 miles, pass a spur trail down to Buck Lake. Just a few feet ahead, intersect the north end of Buck Lake Loop Trail. Potential campsites are about. Cross sandy Buck Lake access road just ahead, keeping west in sand pine scrub. Work your way toward big Farles Prairie. At 18.2 miles, cross FR

30 and reach Farles Prairie. Note the picnic tables left over from the former campground. Head right from FR 30, easterly, passing easy water access and boat ramp. Get the easy water while you can. Turn north along the view-laden edge of prairie. Look for potential campsites in live oaks. Sometimes water is near and sometimes far, depending on annual water levels. At 20.5 miles, come to campsites with marshes on both sides of trail. The prairie here can be comprised of several different ponds. Circle around the right side of Farles Prairie.

At 21.7 miles, cross the site of an old boat ramp. At 21.9 miles, leave Farles Prairie. Campsites can be found hereabouts. The Florida Trail rises north from the prairie to cross FR 30 at 22.4 miles. Next roller-coaster through prototypical sand pine hills, with tilting sand pines rising above scrubby oaks and lichens. At 25.1 miles, come near a palm stand with potential campsites. At 26.4 miles, reach a fine campsite in live oaks just after a board-walk. There is potential water near the boardwalk, though it can dry up. You will hear road noise from FL 40. At 26.6 miles, cross FL 40, then enter the south end of Juniper Prairie Wilderness. Head west in thick woods of pine and bay trees. At 28.0 miles, complete the backpack as you cross the Juniper Springs Recreation Area entrance road. The fee parking is to your right, beyond the entrance station.

## Mileages

| | |
|---|---|
| 0.0 | Clearwater Lake trailhead |
| 2.2 | 1800s gravesite |
| 2.8 | Cross FR 69 |
| 3.7 | Duck Pond |
| 4.8 | Pass under major power line |
| 5.3 | Glenn Branch, campsites |
| 6.0 | Long boardwalk through wooded swamp |
| 6.7 | Cross FR 539 |
| 8.4 | Cross under a transmission line, potential campsites ahead |
| 10.1 | Alexander Springs spur trail leaves right, campsites |
| 10.4 | Cross FR 69 |
| 11.1 | Cross paved Lake CR 445 |
| 13.5 | Cross paved FL 19 |
| 14.4 | Cross sandy FR 57, Summit Pond, campsites ahead |
| 15.1 | Dora's Pond, water, potential campsites |
| 15.8 | Intersect Buck Lake Loop Trail |
| 16.4 | Spur trail to Buck Lake, cross Buck Lake access road ahead |

18.2   FR 30, southern end of Farles Prairie
20.5   Campsites in live oaks
21.7   Pass site of old boat ramp
21.9   Leave Farles Prairie, campsites.
22.4   Cross FR 30
25.1   Pass conspicuous stand of palms
26.4   Boardwalk, campsite
26.6   Cross paved FL 40
28.0   Juniper Springs Recreation Area

## Good Campsites Can Make or Break a Trip

I was traipsing through the Ocala National Forest on a warm day getting warmer. The sand pines seemed endless, the sand trailbed loose. My mood was darkening faster than the imminent night was falling. The trail descended, and I came upon a grove of live oaks overlooking a quaint pond. Nestled in the oaks sat an inviting campsite. I dropped my pack and sat on a log, concluding that, when backpacking, an appealing camp is as important as appealing scenery and weather.

Minimally speaking, a backcountry campsite requires two things: a flat spot and accessible water (although you can carry a limited amount of water for some distance to a campsite). Beyond those two necessities, look for characteristics of the land that will help you deal with the situations at hand. For example, you may want an open, breezy location if insects are troublesome. Or you may want a sheltered location if the winds are howling. You may want shade if it is hot. Or ample fallen wood for a fire if it is cold. Find surroundings that enhance your comfort in camp.

Raising the bar, begin looking for other characteristics that will make your campsite not only functionally desirable but also aesthetically appealing. Why not go for a view if you can get it? Or look over a wildflower garden? Perhaps camp within walking distance of a pond or stream. Discerning backpackers will camp near such highlights, but not too close, to preserve the highlight.

Some backpacking destinations have designated campsites that require a permit such as some Florida state parks, or have specific camping rules. Other places, like national forests, are more freewheeling. Many others have designated campsites that you can stay at without a permit. Check into specific camping regulations *before* your backpacking trip.

Also consider campsite safety. Look around for widow-makers—dead standing trees that may fall during a storm. This actually happened on a backpacking trip I took in Alaska. My friend Scott Davis and I were camped in an aspen grove, one of which fell from wind throw around dawn. Luckily the tree, while falling, hit other trees and was slowed while plunging down onto Scott's shelter. We considered ourselves very lucky.

Don't set your campsite near a stream prone to flooding. Consider an exit strategy. Will you have to ford the river to get back to civilization? If heavy rain is forecast, hike on to another campsite where you can avoid fords.

Therefore, whether it boasts practicality, aesthetics, or safety, a good campsite can make or break a backcountry trip.

# 20

# Saint Francis Backpack

## Overview

This Ocala National Forest overnighter leads you along the lush bottoms of the St. Johns River, passing an abandoned Old Florida town along the way. The loop presents two established campsites en route, as you traverse pinelands on an old logging berm and then come near the St. Johns River and wind through towering lush hammocks of live oak and palm, in the vicinity of Saint Francis before completing the loop.

**Distance & Configuration**: 7.8-mile balloon loop
**Difficulty**: Easy, trail can be mucky
**Outstanding Features**: Florida history, hammock woods
**Scenery**: 4
**Solitude**: 4
**Family-Friendly**: 3
**Canine-Friendly**: 4
**Fees/Permits**: No fees or permits required
**Best Season**: November through March
**Maps**: Ocala National Forest
**For more info**: Ocala National Forest, Seminole Ranger District, 40929 SR 19, Umatilla, FL 32784, 352-669-3153, https://www.fs.usda.gov/recarea/florida/recarea/?recid=83528
**Finding the Trailhead**: From the intersection of FL 19 and CR 42 in Altoona, drive east on CR 42 for 18.1 miles to Forest Road (FR) 542, where there is a sign for River Forest Group Camp. Turn left on FR 542 and follow it for 0.2 mile to the Saint Francis trailhead on your left. GPS trailhead coordinates: 29.012833, -81.392165

The historic Saint Francis Trail parallels a side channel of the St. Johns River known as the Saint Francis Dead River, through a variety of eye-catching habitats en route to the former riverside settlement of Saint Francis. Once a thriving river port connected to the outside world by steamboat traffic, Saint

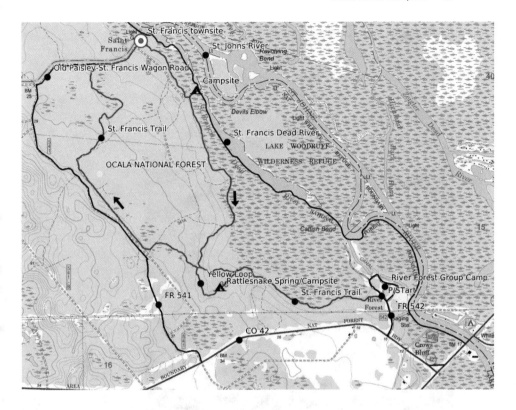

Francis was a trading post where timber and citrus swapped hands for finished goods used by local settlers. Once a railroad was laid through nearby Deland, steamboat shipping died off. By 1935, Saint Francis was completely abandoned. Although the forests have reclaimed the area, you can still see evidence of the old settlements along the way.

Backpackers usually execute this as a one-night adventure, though it could be stretched to two nights. Campsites are limited due to thick and boggy forests. The first campsite established is located near Rattlesnake Spring shortly into the trek; the other is on an old elevated berm next to the river. Additionally, you could search for dry spots in the hammocks near the old landing of Saint Francis.

Be prepared for potentially muddy trail conditions on the second half of the hike. I recommend overnighting here in cool, dry conditions, cutting down on the mosquitoes and muck. Start your backpack by leaving the trailhead kiosk and following the Saint Francis Trail west to cross a small creek. There has been a bridge here in the past and may be in the future. Beyond there, note the regular undulations in the ground, leftover remnants of row crop cultivation. Enter a forest thick with sweetgum and red maple trees. At

Boardwalking through a palm hammock toward Saint Francis.

0.4 mile, traverse the first of many boardwalks spanning forested wetlands of live oak and cabbage palm.

A bridge and boardwalk over another creek precede the junction with the lower end of the Yellow Loop at 1.1 miles. Turn left here, soon coming to another footbridge spanning a small stream. Just upstream of the footbridge is Rattlesnake Spring. Note the sulfurous water bubbling up from the sand of the creek bottom. Campsites are located on either side of the creek here, with dry ground under arching oaks and auburn pines.

Beyond Rattlesnake Spring, the Yellow Loop winds through wet areas on boardwalks and then veers north to intersect the Saint Francis Trail at 1.6 miles. Stay left here, coming to an old logging railroad grade at 2.1 miles. The Saint Francis Trail stretches arrow straight. It is hard to imagine a logging train chugging through here with today's verdant vegetation, once again demonstrating the miraculous recuperative powers of nature.

Leave the berm and meander amid open slash pine flatwoods and low palmetto. The trees are widely spaced, and the sun can blare down. Briefly traverse an oak strand while crossing a stream at 3.7 miles.

Emerge onto a jeep road, the old Paisley–Saint Francis Wagon Road, at 4.3 miles. Trail-less Alexander Springs Wilderness extends to your left. Stay with the jeep road as it leads 0.4 mile to the St. Johns River. The buildings of Saint Francis once lined this road, and the docks for the steamboat were at the end of the road on the river. However, before reaching the river, watch on the right for the blazed trail leaving right from the road. After visiting the old dock site, backtrack from the river and join the blazed trail entering an oak and palm hammock.

Once on the foot trail, look on your left for an artesian spring flowing to the river. Watch for side trails leading to relics of the old town hereabouts. The official trail will be blazed. Solitude seekers can look for camping areas in this vicinity. At 5.3 miles, a wide side trail leads left along an old bridge berm down to the water and a campsite. This linear camp is shaded on both sides of the berm and overlooks a narrow segment of the Saint Francis Dead River, so named because the channel dead-ends rather than rejoining the St. Johns River. Beyond here, camping potential is limited by moist forest.

After the campsite, the Saint Francis Trail traces an old dike erected to flood the land for rice cultivation. The dike forms a division: floodplain forest stretches to your left and pine flatwoods rises to your right. Follow the trail south down the dike until it comes to a stream meander at 5.7 miles. There should be either an official bridge or homemade span. Briefly enter pines before returning to the floodplain forest, where the footpath can be muddy.

Skirt another pine plantation and boardwalks before coming to a trail junction at 6.4 miles. The upper end of the Yellow Loop is just a few steps to your right. Stay left with the Staint Francis Trail under cabbage palm and live oaks. Cross another small stream before intersecting the lower Yellow Loop at 6.7 miles. From here, backtrack to the trailhead, completing the backpack at 7.8 miles.

## Mileages

- 0.0  Saint Francis trailhead
- 1.1  Go left with Yellow Loop
- 1.2  Rattlesnake Spring/campsite
- 4.3  Old Paisley–Saint Francis Wagon Road
- 5.3  Riverside berm campsite
- 7.8  Saint Francis trailhead

# 21

# Seminole State Forest Backpack

## Overview

Make a gorgeous loop incorporating the Florida Trail and other pathways in wildlife-rich Seminole State Forest, northeast of Orlando. Begin on the Florida Trail and then join the Lower Wekiva Loop, skirting the Wekiva River bottoms under majestic oak/palm hammocks. Cross pinelands to reach dark Black Water Creek. The return route rejoins the Florida Trail, winding among pines and oak scrub. Three reservable backcountry campsites—including one trail shelter—enhance the circuit.

**Distance & Configuration**: 11.4-mile loop
**Difficulty**: Moderate
**Outstanding Features**: Trail shelter, Black Water Creek, good campsites
**Scenery**: 5
**Solitude**: 2
**Family-Friendly**: 3
**Canine-Friendly**: 4
**Fees/Permits**: Camping fee plus daily parking permit required
**Best Season**: Late October through mid-April
**Maps**: Seminole State Forest
**For More Info**: Seminole State Forest, 9610 CR 44, Leesburg, FL 34788, 352-360-6675, https://www.fdacs.gov/; Campsite reservations: https://www.reserveamerica.com/, 877-879-3859
**Finding the Trailhead**: From exit 101C on I-4 west of Sanford, take FL 46 west for 5.3 miles to exit right to the signed Bear Pond trailhead. The Florida Trail starts at the east side of the trailhead parking area. GPS trailhead coordinates: 28.815726, -81.426240

Seminole State Forest is a critical tract of land providing a wildlife corridor linking preserved lands both south and north of the Orlando metroplex.

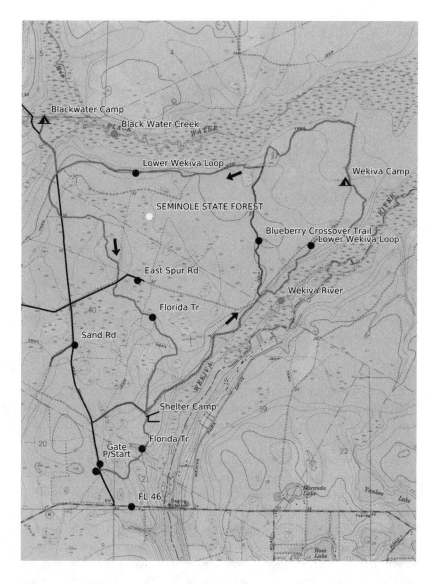

Known for its bears and attractive streams, Seminole State Forest, more than 28,000 acres strong, also links the Florida Trail with points north and south. The Florida Trail forms the backbone of a fine trail system here. The three backcountry campsites along this loop each offer something different, and all are reservable through https://www.reserveamerica.com/. Shelter Camp, set in a pine-bordered clearing, offers a trail shelter to escape the elements (I overnighted here in a driving rainstorm during my thru-hike of the Florida

This is one of the most amenity-laden backcountry campsites in the state.

Trail). Remote Wekiva Camp is situated in a high-canopied live oak/palm hammock, and Black Water Camp is set on the banks of its namesake creek. Most backpackers make this a one-night endeavor, though a two-nighter can be easily done if staying at Shelter Camp the first night, less than a mile from the trailhead.

The trail system is well marked and maintained, making a fine trip for those who want to focus on the experience and not continual navigation. Remember, you must obtain an overnight parking permit in addition to the camping permit. Call the forest office to obtain the parking permit.

Leave the Bear Pond trailhead on the Florida Trail, a single-track path, eastbound in pine/palmetto/scrub oak flatwoods. Hodgepodge oak copses intermingle with tawny pines. Cross a boardwalk over a stream seep at 0.5 mile, then, at 0.8 mile, reach Shelter Camp. The three-sided open-fronted refuge dominates a clearing that also has picnic tables, benches, and a fire ring. Bring your own water. The clearing presents numerous tent sites. The shelter, one of but a few along the Florida Trail, is heavily used as a stopping/picnic area by day hikers, so expect visitors aplenty when camping here on weekends.

The Florida Trail continues past Shelter Camp, nearing a sand road and then turning right to reach an intersection at 0.9 mile. Here, the Florida

Trail, your return route, splits left, whereas our circuit stays right, joining the Lower Wekiva Loop. Head northeast, often skirting the divide between upland pines with palmetto prairies to your left, and lush, moist hammocks of palm and live oaks dripping Spanish moss sloping to the Wekiva River. Just a few feet in elevation in Florida can make the difference between sun-burnished low scrub and towering hardwood jungles; you'll hike through both here.

At 2.3 miles, the Blueberry Crossover Trail leaves left, shortcutting the circuit. Keep northeast in hammock woods. The path becomes rooty and sometimes mucky under sweetgum, maple, and live oaks. At 2.6 miles, a boardwalk leads across a small tributary. Continue winding between open pinelands, scrub oaks, and hardwood hammocks. At 3.8 miles, the Lower Wekiva Loop emerges onto an elevated double-track in moist woods. Turn right here, joining the double-track, and then find the spur to Wekiva Camp just ahead on your left. This small campsite features a picnic table, fire ring, and benches ensconced in tall palms over which rise taller live oaks, fashioning a shady camp. Tent sites are limited. Bring your own water. I recommend this camp during colder times to mitigate the mosquito potential.

The Lower Wekiva Loop thankfully stays on the elevated berm through soggy woods, abruptly turning left, west, at 4.3 miles. Continue in tall live oak–dominated woods, now paralleling Black Water Creek to your right. At 5.3 miles, reach the other end of the Blueberry Crossover Trail. From here, the Lower Wekiva Loop splits right, running in conjunction with a yellow-blazed equestrian trail (not shown on the map). Stay with the double-track, westbound, opening onto widely scattered pines, almost a palmetto prairie. The trailbed can be sandy here.

At 7.0 miles, come to hard-packed Sand Road, open only to private drivers who have a forest permit. Join Sand Road right, northbound. The Florida Trail follows Sand Road. The walking is easy. At 7.4 miles, a signed path splits right and shortly dead-ends on Black Water Creek at Black Water Camp. Here, you will find a campsite on an elevated track overlooking Black Water Creek. It has a picnic table, benches, a fire ring, and slightly sloped tent sites. If you cannot find the correct spur to Black Water Camp, hike Sand Road to the bridge over Black Water Creek, then backtrack. The correct spur is the first spur heading south from the bridge.

From Black Water Camp, backtrack 0.4 mile down Sand Road to where the Florida Trail splits from Sand Road. Begin winding through widely dispersed pines, mostly on single-track trail. Have your hat ready, as much of this is open to the sun. Cross Sand Road at 8.2 miles. Keep mostly south on a packed sand track, sometimes hiking through low oak scrub thickets. Pass a small marsh pond at 8.5 miles. The Florida Trail crosses East Spur Road at 9.1 miles, then enters a longleaf pine restoration area. True to the mission, longleaf pines are rising overhead. The walking remains easy as the restoration area gives way to oak and sand pine scrub before you complete the loop portion of the hike at 10.5 miles. From here, backtrack past Shelter Camp, reaching the trailhead at 11.4 miles.

## Mileages

- 0.0   Bear Pond parking area
- 0.8   Shelter Camp
- 3.9   Wekiva Camp
- 7.0   North on Sand Road
- 7.4   Black Water Camp
- 10.5   Complete loop
- 11.4   Bear Pond parking area

# 22

St. Johns River Backpack

## Overview

This easy one-night backpack takes you to some alluring campsites along the banks of the St. Johns River, within the confines of Lake Monroe Conservation Area. An easy trek, the adventure leads you past ponds before entering a rich tree hammock only to traverse more open terrain. Make your way to the St. Johns River at Brickyard Slough, where a set of campsites are situated on a wooded and scenic river bend.

**Distance & Configuration**: 4.0-mile there-and-back
**Difficulty**: Easy
**Outstanding Features**: Great campsites, family backpack
**Scenery**: 4
**Solitude**: 2
**Family-Friendly**: 5
**Canine-Friendly**: 5
**Fees/Permits**: None
**Best Season**: Mid-October through April
**Maps**: Lake Monroe Conservation Area
**For More Info**: St. Johns Water Management District, Bayard Field Station, PO Box 1429, Palatka, FL 32178, 904-529-2381, https://www.sjrwmd.com/
**Finding the Trailhead**: From exit 108 on I-4 near Deltona, take Debary Avenue east for 1.9 miles, then continue east as Debary Avenue becomes Doyle Road. Drive 1.3 miles farther, then turn right onto Garfield Road. Follow it 0.9 mile to turn left onto Osteen Enterprises Road. Follow it 2.2 miles, to veer right onto Reed Ellis Road, following it for 2.2 miles to meet FL 415. Here, cross FL 415 to enter Beck Ranch Park, then turn right just after passing through the park roundabout and open onto a large parking area. The Red Trail starts at the far end of the large parking area. GPS trailhead coordinates: 28.820152, -81.184353

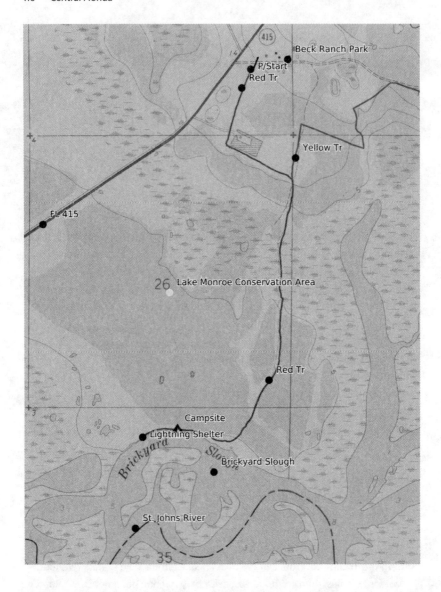

In parts of Florida they swim with the dolphins, but at Lake Monroe Conservation Area we backpack with the cattle. (There has been an ongoing cattle-grazing lease here, so you may see cows on the hike.) The former ranch, acquired by St. Johns Water Management District back in 1987, lies in a pretty part of Volusia County. Now known as Lake Monroe Conservation Area, the tract preserves part of the Lake Monroe and St. Johns River drainage, enhancing water quality and adding flood protection for the St. Johns River watershed.

Your view while camping here at Lake Monroe Conservation Area.

The backcountry camping area, set in a live oak hammock along a curving shoreline of Brickyard Slough, is the highlight of the overnighting experience here. In fact, the hike is quite easy, save for one possible wet crossing of an overflow drainage of a pond.

Since the hike is short and laid-back, pack weight is not as much of a concern as for other hikes; you may want to bring extra goodies, such as tasty food treats, spare clothes, etc. Leave south from the large parking area on the Red Trail, with a pair of large dug ponds to your left and FL 415 to your right. You are in open terrain on a grassy track. At 0.3 mile, the Red Trail turns left along a fence line then comes to the pesky outflow of the pond to your left. At low water the concrete ford could be dry, but if not, simply take off your shoes, cross the spot, then put your shoes back on. This is the only likely foot wetting of the entire trip.

The wet crossing eliminates 90 percent of casual day hikers. You are now hiking easterly on an elevated grassy track to meet the Yellow Trail at 0.6 miles. Here, turn right with the Red Trail, dipping into moist hammock woods of palm and live oak. Shortly pop out back in grasses with scattered tree islands near and far. At 1.6 miles, the waters of the St. Johns River and Brickyard Slough come into view. Curve right here, coming along the shoreline, where scattered palms add to the scenery with the live oak hammock curving with the curve of Brickyard Slough.

At 1.7 miles, come to the first of several, first-come, first-served campsites (paddlers and boaters can access the campsites as well, creating competition on nice winter weekends). The camps offer picnic table, upright grill, bench, and fire ring. Water is available from the St. Johns. Enjoy the view from the campsites of marshy wetlands and waters, with rich woods at your back. Continue along the water's edge, passing the other campsites until reaching a wooden lightning shelter at 2.0 miles. Beyond here the shoreline gives way to marsh. After enjoying an evening here, it is a simple backtrack to the trailhead.

## Mileages

0.0   Trailhead
2.0   Brickyard Slough campsites
4.0   Trailhead

### Backpackers Have Food Choices

Inquisitive outdoor enthusiasts often ask me, "What do you eat while backpacking?" The answer: "It depends." What type of trip am I going on? How long is it? I want foods that have as little water weight as possible, are packaged for travel, nutritious (or at least filling), and easy to make. Place a grain of salt in your pack when you read this and don't blame me for food poisoning.

When I started backpacking, I tried freeze-dried meals. Generally coming in foil pouches to which you add boiling water and wait, freeze-dried meals are tastier than they used to be, but they are pricey and no fun to cook. After questioning the freeze-dried status quo, I brought my indoor pantry outdoors.

First, why the paranoia about spoiled food? If it smells bad, don't eat it. Few backpacking trips last longer than a week, and most trips just a weekend. So why eat like a Florida Trail thru-hiker?

**Breakfast**: Simple Quaker oats are light and filling. Traditional long-cooking oats taste better and are more nutritious than individual packets. Raisins lend flavor and add some nutritious fruit to your wilderness diet. Other lightweight breakfasts include country ham, bagels, and cream cheese. I make my own cereal and mix it with reconstituted dried milk.

**The base of my lunches**: flat flour tortillas. Think of tortillas as presmashed bread. Other packable breads include bagels, English muffins, and pita bread. Add peanut butter and fruit preserves to make a roll-up sandwich. You have to work to get fruit into an outback diet. Or put in smoked oysters and add mozzarella slices to munch a nice greasy, filling lunch.

To meat or not to meat? (If you are vegetarian, skip to the **Cheese** paragraph.) Even on the trail, my first night's fare features heavy perishables to cook over hot coals, such as hamburgers, chicken breasts, or steak and whole baked potatoes or baked onions. Microwave the taters or onions at home, then wrap in foil after smearing them with butter and spices. Reheat in coals. If you are suspicious about meat going bad, do this: freeze it at home, wrap it in foil, and it will be thawed by the time you arrive at camp. Also, consider premade salad kits for some first-night greenery.

Spam and Vienna sausages are no-brainers, so let's skip to hot dogs, kielbasa, and other precooked links. You would think that kielbasa and hot dogs are for the first or second night, but they will keep up to a week. Salami and summer sausages are good choices that don't require refrigeration.

**Cheese**: My tests show that cream cheese keeps well not refrigerated. Regular cheese keeps pretty well, too. It might get a little greasy or malformed in warmer weather, but it neither scares me nor makes me sick. Also consider string cheese or wax-covered cheese.

**Snacks**: trail mix, jelly beans, nuts, or sardines. Don't forget the bars—candy, granola, nutrition or energy bars. Other standards, like beef jerky and dried fruit, are standards for a reason. They work. They're light.

Backpackers often carry easy dinners—macaroni and cheese, instant mashed potatoes, couscous, stuffing, rice. The most important thing is your backcountry experience. There's no reason you can't enjoy what you normally eat, and even look to it as a reward at the end of a hard day. After all, "an army travels on its stomach"... well, so does a backpacker.

# 23

## Citrus Loop Backpack

### Overview

Using a series of connected loops, make a long circuit backpack at the varied Citrus Tract of the Withlacoochee State Forest. Leave Holder Mine Campground and then roll through pine and turkey oak–clad hills to a fine first night's camp in oaks. Next head south in hilly forest, passing a second campsite before entering a land of rocky sinks and ponds, with even bigger hills. Find another camp in the most southerly part of the forest. Your final day turns back north, passing near Mutual Mine Campground before joining an old railroad grade that leads you back to the trailhead.

---

**Distance & Configuration**: 32.4-mile loop, can be shortened
**Difficulty**: Difficult due to distance
**Outstanding Features**: Big circuit, geology, good campsites
**Scenery**: 5
**Solitude**: 3
**Family-Friendly**: 1
**Canine-Friendly**: 3
**Fees/Permits**: No fees or permits required
**Best Season**: November through late April
**Maps**: Withlacoochee State Forest; Citrus Hiking Trails Brochure
**For more info**: Withlacoochee State Forest, 15003 Broad St, Brooksville, FL 34601-4201, 352-797-4140, https://www.fdacs.gov/
**Finding the Trailhead**: From exit 329 on I-75 east of Inverness, take FL 44 west for 16.7 miles; then turn left onto Pleasant Grove Road just west of downtown Inverness. Follow Pleasant Grove Road for 2.5 miles, turning right onto Forest Road (FR) 10 toward Holder Mine Campground. After 1.8 miles, pass Holder Mine Campground on your right and then quickly look left for the signed trailhead parking area. GPS trailhead coordinates: 28.799471, -82.383878

---

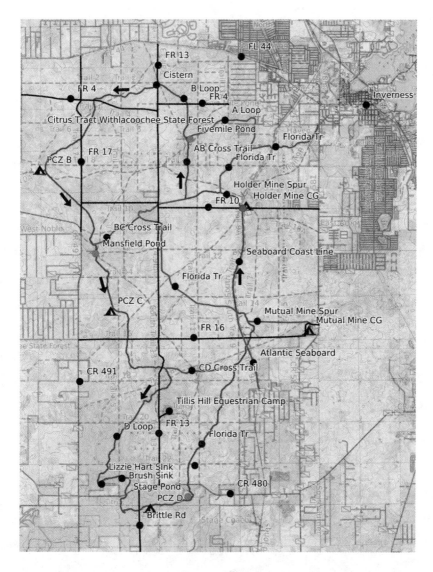

With every day that passes, the Citrus Tract of the Withlacoochee State Forest becomes more valuable as civilization creeps closer to the 50,000-acre parcel of Central Florida where hilly pinelands, moist live oak hammocks, and rocky sinks establish the backdrop over which a series of four connected hiker-only loop trails create a backpacking circuit that can extend from a few miles to more than 40 miles. The adventure outlined here makes for a good two- to three-night trip that explores the Citrus Tract from one end to the other.

The author trekking through a recent prescribed burn.

Here are some things to remember: Hikers must camp in the designated "primitive camping zones" outlined on the map. Holder Mine Campground, where this backpack starts, is the preferred parking area for backpackers. Water is generally not available at the campsites. Therefore, you must get it from limited sources in the forest and then carry it or cache your water at forest road crossings. Caching is the better option. However, this requires driving on some of the sand fire roads that lace the forest. Be careful—some of the lesser forest roads require four-wheel drive. Also, check the state forest website for hunt dates, and wear orange when warranted. Finally, the state forest regularly uses prescribed fire, so expect to travel through recent burns at some point.

Generally speaking, the Citrus Tract is a high, dry parcel with more hills than swamps. If you do this whole loop, you experience just over 2,000 feet of elevation gain/loss, serious ups and downs by Florida standards. Under normal conditions, backpacking here should be a dry-footed affair. Campsites cannot be reserved. They each have fire ring and benches. Your adventure will utilize a portion of the famed Florida Trail along with more of the Citrus Trail, broken into loops. The trails are well maintained and blazed. Signs are posted at major intersections. The scenery is good throughout. You won't be disappointed.

Leave west on FR 10 from the Holder Mine trailhead parking, traveling 253 feet before splitting right on a blue-blazed hiker trail linking the campground to the Florida Trail. Roll over your first hills of the trip, then meet the Florida Trail at 0.8 mile. Head left here, southbound, on the Florida Trail. At 1.4 miles, cross FR 11. The Citrus Tract has a dizzying number of official and unofficial forest roads, as well as road-like equestrian trails (not all forest roads are shown on accompanying map), but look on the backs of signs at the sand road crossings where the forest roads are usually labeled. Roll into scrub and turkey oaks under a superstory of pines.

At 1.8 miles, split right, away from the Florida Trail, heading north on the A-B Cross Trail, crossing FR 10A at 2.2 miles, and FR 8 at 2.5 miles, in hilly terrain. At 3.1 miles, dip into a live oak hammock with mucky Fivemile Pond to your right. Pass a shaded picnic bench and then meet the other end of the A Loop. From here, stay straight, now on the B Loop, undulating through pines, wiregrass, and turkey oaks. At 3.7 miles, cross FR 6; and at 4.2 miles, cross FR 4. At 5.0 miles, come to FR 13. This is a good place to cache water, as FR 13 is kept in passable shape. A square water cistern stands next to the road. This locale is among the tract's highest elevations, breaking 150 feet just ahead. Traverse evergreens, crossing FR 15 at 6.1 miles. Keep westerly and cross FR 4 a second time at 6.8 miles. The hills just keep on rolling, cloaked in scrub live oaks and pines. At 9.2 miles, rise to an intersection. Here, a short spur goes right to PCZ (primitive camping zone) B, also known as Jackson Camp. It is located in an oak dome encircled by pines, with ample tent sites, on a slight slope.

Resume the loop, crossing FR 17 again at 10.8 miles. This is a decent water caching spot. At 11.9 miles, reach an intersection. Here, the BC Cross Trail goes left toward Holder Mine while we keep south, now on the C Loop in tall pines, with an understory of scattered scrub oaks. Dip to a hardwood hammock and circle around willowy Mansfield Pond, shaded by towering live oaks. Rise from the thicket back into pine, oak scrub, and wiregrass ecosystem, with scattered oak domes. At 13.7 miles, reach the signed short spur right to less-used PCZ C, aka Youngblood Camp, set in a mix of live oaks and pines.

From the camp, continue south in turkey oaks and pines through sandy hills. Cross FR 16 at 14.9 miles. It is when crossing the sand forest roads that you will either enter or exit recent burns. Work through a sink with exposed rock and bigger oaks draped with resurrection ferns just before crossing FR 13 at 16.4 miles. Here, the CD Cross Trail keeps left while we split right on D Loop, rising to pine oak scrub. In an oak hammock forest, at 17.1 miles, cross FR 13 again, keeping southwest. At this point be aware of crossing horse trails (not shown on the map) as well as forest roads. However, the blazed hiking trails are simple to follow.

The hills increase and the woods get thicker as you enter richer soils, with cedars and maple trees. At 19.6 miles, cross FR 22 and then reach a rocky dry sink on your left. The stone mouth leads to a cave entrance of sorts. From there, drop off hills to circle around rocky and lushly vegetated Lizzie Hart Sink. Rocks abound. Ferns carpet the magnolia-, sycamore-, and hickory-rich area. This is an abundant wildflower area in spring. Climb away to cross FR 15 and then dip to pass the less dramatic Brush Sink at 21.1 miles. The trail turns south to cross paved CR 480 at 21.7 miles.

Run through hills, then come along a gullied stream that ends in a sink at 22.6 miles. Rise to cross Brittle Road at 22.8 miles. This is a good place to cache water. Continue rising in hardwood- and evergreen-clad hills to reach the spur trail right to PCZ D, also known as Taylor Camp, at 23.1 miles. This heavily used, slightly sloped site is shaded by pines, oaks, and palm. Beyond here, continue in thick rocky woods, easterly, descending toward Stage Pond, a large partly vegetated body of water. Circle around Stage Pond in thick oak woods. Ahead, split abruptly right, climbing into pines to cross paved CR 480 again at 24.7 miles. Here, you rejoin the Florida Trail, northbound in piney woods. Ahead, you will cross multiple forest roads and equestrian tracks. Cross FR 22 at 25.5 miles, and FR 18 at 27.7 miles.

At 28.0 miles, reach the east end of the CD Cross Trail. Keep straight on the orange-blazed Florida Trail. At 28.7 miles, cross the elevated berm of the old Seaboard Coast Line (other sections of this line comprise the Withlacoochee State Trail, Florida's longest rail trail). You will be rejoining this abandoned rail line later, but for now stick with the Florida Trail, crossing FR 16 at 28.9 miles. At 29.5 miles, intersect the elevated Mutual Mine Spur, which leaves right 1.5 miles to Mutual Mine Campground, with water and developed campsites. Keep straight, still with the Florida Trail.

At 29.9 miles, split right with the Seaboard Coast Line former line, after crossing FR 9A. It is paralleled by FR 9 on the far side. You can distinguish the old rail line from forest roads because the rail line is kept level by cutting through hills and staying on elevated berms above low spots. Unfortunately, where the seaboard cuts through hills ATVs have created sandy ruts while climbing the hills. Nevertheless, the hard-packed Seaboard Coast Line makes for a good route, keeping northbound. At 31.4 miles, dip to cross FR 12. Continue north, straight, reaching FR 10 and hike's end at 32.4 miles, completing a first-rate Florida backpacking adventure. The parking area is just to your right.

## Mileages

| | |
|---|---|
| 0.0 | Holder Mine trailhead |
| 0.8 | Left on Florida Trail |
| 1.8 | Right on AB Cross Trail |
| 3.1 | Left on B Loop |
| 5.0 | Cross FR 13, cistern |
| 9.2 | Spur to PCZ B |
| 11.9 | BC Cross Trail goes left |
| 13.7 | Spur right to PCZ C |
| 21.7 | Cross paved CR 480 |
| 23.1 | Spur right to PCZ D |
| 24.7 | Cross paved CR 480, join Florida Trail |
| 28.0 | Pass east end of CD Cross Trail |
| 29.5 | Mutual Mine Spur leaves right |
| 29.9 | Split right with old Seaboard Coast Line |
| 32.4 | Holder Mine trailhead |

# 24

## Croom Tract Backpack

### Overview

This circuit backpack in the Withlacoochee State Forest presents two designated campsites amid its pine and oak woods, with a little added surprise. Start at the popular Tucker Hill trailhead and then make your counterclockwise circuit, rolling through pines. Join the Florida Trail, reaching the first designated backcountry campsite under sand live oaks. From there, skirt bottomlands of the Withlacoochee River before tackling some bona fide Florida hills. The final part of the trek leads past a second campsite before climbing Tucker Hill.

---

**Distance & Configuration**: 11.3-mile loop
**Difficulty**: Moderate
**Outstanding Features**: Good campsites, hills
**Scenery**: 4
**Solitude**: 2
**Family-Friendly**: 3
**Canine-Friendly**: 5
**Fees/Permits**: Daily parking permit required
**Best Season**: Late October through late April
**Maps**: Withlacoochee State Forest—Croom Tract Hiking Trails
**For More Info**: Withlacoochee State Forest, 15003 Broad St, Brooksville, FL 34601-4201, 352-797-4140, https://www.fdacs.gov/
**Finding the Trailhead**: From exit 301 on I-75 near Brooksville, take US 98 south/FL 50 east for 1.1 miles to turn left on Croom Rital Road. Follow it for 5.6 miles and then stay left on CR 480 west/Croom Road. Drive for 3.9 miles to the hiker/mountain biker parking area on your left. GPS trailhead coordinates: 28.593730, -82.296042

---

The Croom Tract of the Withlacoochee State Forest near Brooksville is the setting for this loop backpack that features two quality backcountry

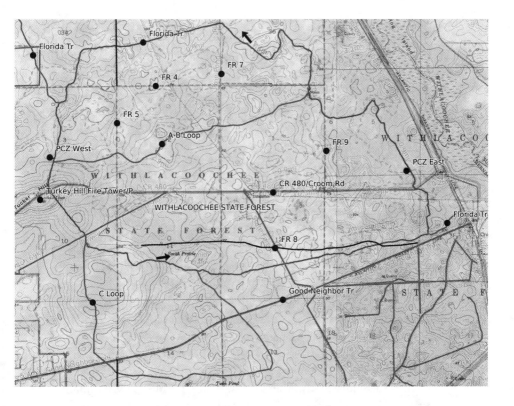

campsites and a variety of environments through which to hike. Bordered on the east by the scenic Withlacoochee River, the Croom Tract rises westward from the floodplain live oak hammocks along the river, to mixed pine oak woods, and, higher still, to pine/turkey oak forests gracing mounds and swales rising farther to dare-I-say "Florida mountains" that enhance the scenery and add vertical variation to the circuit.

The backpack uses designated hiker-only trails, including a stretch of the Florida Trail. You will encounter separate networks of equestrian and mountain biking paths (not shown on the map), but each of the trail systems is well marked and maintained, eliminating confusion and cross-use of paths when they intersect. Campsites are first-come, first-served, but you must pay the daily forest use fee. The camps offer a picnic table, fire ring, and tent sites, but you must bring your own water. Fortunately, the backpack crosses forest roads that allow you to cache water near the camps, easing the burden of toting aqua.

The trailside scenery will please the eye. Leave the Tucker Hill hiker and mountain biker parking area, passing through a shaded picnic area to head south on the yellow-blazed B Loop hiking trail. Head south in scrubby

Relaxing by the fire on a chilly January morn.

pine-oak-sweetgum woods. You soon start rolling in lightly undulating forest, complete with a few rocks here and there. Cross a power line and reach a trail intersection at 0.7 mile. Here, head left with the B-C Loop, cutting through a disturbed area to enter pine woods. Cross sandy Forest Road (FR) 5 at 1.0 mile. Official sand forest roads are well used compared to grown-over fire lanes and other woods tracks you will encounter. Continue in rolling pines. Some of the lower, moister swales are cloaked in oaks. At 1.9 miles, the C Loop comes in on your right. Keep straight in oak woods, passing Smith Prairie on your left. At 2.2 miles, cross FR 7.

At 3.2 miles, bisect FR 9. Cruise the margin between oak thickets and pines. Ahead cross FR 8. Look through the woods to your right for the paved Good Neighbor Multi-Use Trail. At 4.3 miles, meet the Florida Trail. Turn north, left, here in thicker, moister forest, running parallel to the Withlacoochee River bottoms. Look for hickories along the path, then pass by a cypress swamp. Cut across the power line clearing before crossing paved Croom Road at 4.8 miles.

This is a good place to cache water if staying at PCZ East, on a short spur left at 5.0 miles. The level camp is located in a low sand live oak dome bordered with pines and is complemented by picnic table and fire ring. Tent sites are ample. A mountain biking trail rolls nearby. From here, the

Florida Trail continues north in a mosaic of woods, primarily pines. Tramp alongside a couple of marsh ponds before crossing FR 9 at 6.4 miles. The Withlacoochee State Forest is actively burned, and the forest roads are used to block off burn areas, often resulting in widely varying forests altered at the cross of a sand track.

The trail becomes a little hillier and takes you by an old mine, now wooded, at 6.8 miles. Just ahead, the A-B Loop splits left if you want to shortcut the circuit. Stay with the Florida Trail, crossing FR 4 at 7.1 miles. Enter hill country. And the Florida Trail rightfully takes you to and over some sloped terrain, giving you a taste of the leg burn experienced by Appalachian Mountain backpackers. The views may not be as distant, but you can still lord over the valleys below.

Cross FR 7 at 8.5 miles. Continue tackling hills before bisecting FR 5 at 9.6 miles. The hills ease up as you wander west in pines. Turn south, crossing FR 4 at 10.3 miles. At 10.5 miles, a fainter Florida Trail splits right, northbound, while you join the more-used A Loop. At 11.1 miles, while climbing a bit, look right for the spur to PCZ West. It is located in a pine stand, with picnic table, fire ring, benches, and tent sites. Ahead, intersect the other end of the A-B Cross Trail. Climb toward the crest of Tucker Hill, elevation 181 feet, crossing Croom Road and completing the backpack at 11.3 miles.

## Mileages

| | |
|---|---|
| 0.0 | Tucker Hill hiker/mountain biker parking area |
| 0.7 | Left with B-C Loop |
| 4.3 | Left with Florida Trail |
| 5.0 | PCZ East |
| 10.5 | Leave Florida Trail |
| 11.1 | PCZ West |
| 11.3 | Tucker Hill hiker/mountain biker parking area |

# 25

## Richloam Loop Backpack

### Overview

This scenic and challenging circuit explores a lowland segment of the Withlacoochee State Forest. First, curve past the bottoms of the Withlacoochee River. Then wend your way through wild lands to saddle alongside silent, dark Little Withlacoochee River before working through bright, open, grassy ponds. Three designated campsites are situated along the eye-pleasing loop.

---

**Distance & Configuration**: 27.5-mile loop
**Difficulty**: Moderate-difficult
**Outstanding Features**: Swamp forests, big loop
**Scenery**: 4
**Solitude**: 3
**Family-Friendly**: 1
**Canine-Friendly**: 3
**Fees/Permits**: No fees or permit required
**Best Season**: Late December through early April
**Maps**: Withlacoochee State Forest; Richloam Hiking Trail Brochure
**For more info**: Withlacoochee State Forest, 15003 Broad St, Brooksville, FL 34601-4201, 352-797-4140, https://www.fdacs.gov/
**Finding the Trailhead**: From exit 301 on I-75 east of Brooksville, take US 98 south/FL 50 east exit, and stay with FL 50 for 7.5 miles to turn right onto Porter Gap Road (there will be a sign for Richloam General Store here.) Follow Porter Gap Road for 0.5 mile, continuing a little beyond Richloam General Store to the trailhead on your right. GPS trailhead coordinates: 28.500171, -82.112665

---

The Richloam Tract of the Withlacoochee State Forest, more than 58,000 acres, is so named for fertile soils of the lowlands around the Withlacoochee and Little Withlacoochee Rivers. Luckily for us, a segment of the Florida

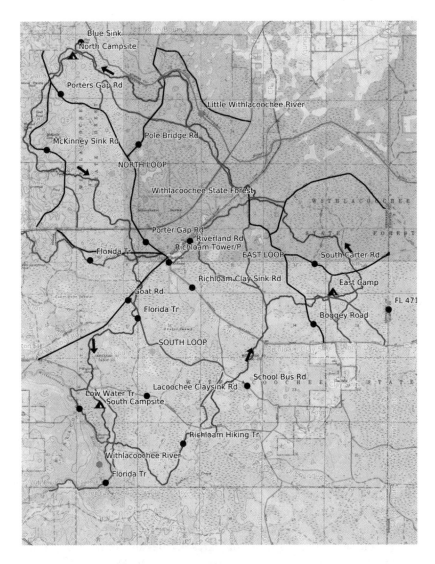

Trail along with the Richloam Hiking Trail and connector trails together form a grand circuit where backpackers can explore the densely wooded tract where cypress swamps, pine forests, and oak halls commingle along with the aforementioned waterways along with grassy depression ponds, a place where wild pigs, deer, and other wildlife roam. Be prepared for potentially soggy trails and an ever-changing thick forestscape. Better to wait until early winter, drying the trails, before backpacking here. Along the way you will cross seemingly innumerable official and unofficial forest roads.

You will experience lowlands, ponds, and small streams throughout this backpack.

Three interconnected loops, almost entirely single-track foot trails, allow you to make circuits of your own choosing, but our route makes the longest possible loop. You can shorten these loops for quick one-night trips, but this should be a two- to three-night exploit. The three designated campsites along the route are first-come, first-served. Water can be had along the trail, but caching water at forest road crossings is a recommended option. Make sure to cache at major forest roads shown on the map; otherwise lesser forest roads may require four-wheel drive and nerves of steel.

Start the backpack at Richloam Fire Tower, erected when the state forest was established in the 1930s, part of a Great Depression federal works project. On the way in, stop at the rustic Richloam General Store, a throwback to the time when this part of Florida was a rural backwater. Do not take the nearest blue-blazed trail from the trailhead; rather, walk Porter Gap Road back toward FL 50, passing Richloam General Store, then split left, joining a single-track, blue-blazed connector trail, westbound to meet the Richloam Hiking Trail at 0.7 mile. Head left in low, moist woods, heavy with laurel oaks and pine. Cypress swamps are never far in this thick, viny forest.

Quickly meet the Florida Trail. Join it, following the orange blazes left as the other leg of the Florida Trail heads west. At 1.2 miles, cross sandy Goat Road, then work through a mucky section to rise into high pines with palmetto. However, pinelands are the exception in Richloam, and ahead you run into oak-dominated forest. At 3.2 miles, bridge a little streamlet, and another at 3.6 miles. At 3.8 miles, cross Lacoochee Claysink Road just before reaching yet another trail intersection. Here, the scenic Low Water Trail splits right along the Withlacoochee River, adding 0.3 mile to your hike. However, if you go that way, you miss the recommended South Campsite at 4.2 miles, set on a spur trail under shady oaks. Like all camps here, it offers a fire ring, picnic table, and tent sites.

Continuing the South Loop, pass the other end of the Low Water Trail at 5.0 miles; then the Florida Trail splits right just ahead. Keep straight, on the Richloam Hiking Trail, eastbound. Look for rock outcrops beside depression marshes. You will also near cypress swamps while traversing thick oak woods. Cross Lacoochee Claysink Road again at 7.8 miles. The forest remains thick, especially in moist hardwoods of oak, sweetgum, and maples. Cross School Bus Road at 9.0 miles, then traverse a low hardwood hammock forest of bay, live oak, hickory, and fern gardens. Look for pig tracks here.

Cross Richloam Claysink Road at 9.9 miles. Return to swamp woods and reach a trail junction at 10.3 miles. Head right here, now on the East Loop in pine oak woods (the other end of the East Loop goes left). Swamp forests are never far away. At 11.3 miles, cross Boggey Road. Work through a wet strand before rising to drier pines. At 12.1 miles, a spur leads left to the East Campsite. This not-so-great site is next to a cypress swamp under live oaks. The site as a whole is a little boggy. You may have to pitch your tent on higher ground.

The East Loop continues, crossing South Carter Road at 12.8 miles. Stay in pinewoods with nearby swamps. Cut through a cypress strand at 13.7 miles. Cross North Carter Road at 15.0 miles. Continue west in picturesque live oaks, and at 15.5 miles, a spur trail leads left 1.8 miles to the Richloam trailhead. We keep straight, joining the North Loop. Cross paved River-land Road; then join an elevated old railroad grade south before breaking northeast to cross paved FL 50 at 16.5 miles. Reenter low hammock woods with live oaks. You are now paralleling the swamp-bordered Little Withlacoochee River for the next several miles. The scenery is gorgeous.

At 18.7 miles, pass an access to Pole Bridge Road and keep running parallel to the Little Withlacoochee River. Meet the spur right to Blue Sink at 20.1. Follow it a quarter mile to the duck moss–covered body of water. After visiting the sink, turn south, entering live oak forests rising between a plethora of grassy ponds, more grass than pond, but attractive nonetheless. At 21.6 miles, a spur leads left to recommended North Campsite, set in hardwoods overlooking a grassy pond, where water can be had.

The trail continues winding south between these ponds in laurel oaks, crossing Porters Gap Road at 22.2 miles. Ahead, Richloam Hiking Trail goes on and off old double-tracks. Pay close attention to the blazes here as you continue to wind among the ponds to cross McKinney Sink Road at 24.4 miles. Enjoy dry oak woods with occasional ponds to cross paved FL 50 a second time at 26.3 miles. Keep south to complete the loop at 26.8 miles. From here, it is a 0.7 mile backtrack to the trailhead, passing the Richloam General Store one last time. Stop in. After this backpack you are due a treat!

## Mileages

| | |
|---|---|
| 0.0 | Richloam trailhead |
| 0.7 | Begin Richloam Hiking Trail, join Florida Trail |
| 3.8 | Cross Lacoochee Claysink Road |
| 4.2 | South Campsite |
| 5.0 | Leave Florida Trail |
| 7.8 | Cross Lacoochee Claysink Road |
| 9.9 | Cross Richloam Claysink Road |
| 11.3 | Cross Boggey Road |
| 12.1 | East Campsite |
| 15.5 | Spur left to Richloam trailhead |
| 16.5 | Cross FL 50 |
| 20.1 | Spur to Blue Sink |
| 21.6 | North Campsite |
| 24.4 | Cross McKinney Sink Road |
| 26.3 | Cross FL 50 |
| 27.5 | Richloam trailhead |

### Tent, Netting, Tarp, or under the Stars While Backpacking?

Due to the abundance of insects in the Sunshine State, most backpackers bring a tent with them. Solo backpackers use ultralight single-person models. Multiple backpackers can share a bigger tent—and the weight that goes along with it. However, there are times and situations when a tent isn't needed—or wanted. Whenever possible, I sleep out in the open, under the stars, partly because I am lazy and do not want to carry, set up, or take down a tent. During winter in Florida, cold fronts bring chilly conditions that can negate the bug threat for days. For short trips with a reliable cold weather forecast, I bring no shelter at all, saving weight and space, and get to backpack, camp—and sleep—in the great outdoors. However, on warmer trips the bugs will return after the cold snap is over, thus I bring a mosquito net covering, hung up with a center string and then staked to the ground around my sleeping bag. These mosquito nets are small, lightweight, and a hassle to get into and out of. I hiked the entire Florida Trail with just a mosquito net and poncho for shelter. It was trying at times but was worth the weight savings.

Nevertheless, tents are the time-honored shelter of choice for backpackers. Before pitching a tent, ask yourself why are you staying in a nylon bubble? There are five primary reasons for taking a tent with you: bugs, precipitation, cold, wind, and privacy. A tent will keep the bugs out, the rain away, ease the chill, and block the blows.

Don't underestimate the privacy function of tents. Also, tents can provide mental protection from the dark as well as physical shelter for greenhorn campers. Backpackers have to consider a smaller tent, sacrificing tent space for weight. Be prepared for a tight squeeze when using ultralight tents. Ultralight tents are superthin, so you have to exercise caution with them on the trail, avoiding a tear. Remember, you get what you pay for when buying a tent.

Consider a tarp for rainy days. Tarps can be used as your primary shelter if in the cold or not in bug country. Today's silicon impregnated nylon tarps weigh as little as a pound. Tarps can be configured in a variety of ways, and can also be used for sun protection when at camp. I prefer a 10' × 12' size. Bring plenty of cord to string up your tarp—at least 12 feet for each corner to be on the safe side, with a separate 40-foot cord to string a main line between trees.

Florida backpackers can employ a tarp and bug screen combination. A single-person bug screen weighs mere ounces. Add an ultralightweight tarp. This entire setup is very small, packable, and can weigh less than 1.5 pounds. Getting your mosquito net set up under the tarp can be challenging. Practice setting it up at home before getting out on the trail.

As opposed to tenters, hammock campers have the advantage of not having to find an acceptable flat spot to overnight, but they do need two properly placed trees to string up their haven. Sleeping in a hammock can be comfortable, especially in mild to warm weather. In a hammock the sleeper is exposed to the air all around their body, which can be troublesome in cold conditions. Consider using an "underquilt," a down blanket of sorts that warms your underside, under your pad, in cold weather.

Therefore, when backpacking in Florida, you have a wide variety of shelter options you can use on the trail.

# 26

## Green Swamp West Backpack

### Overview

Follow a section of the Florida Trail through the Green Swamp West Wildlife Management Area (WMA). Start near the Withlacoochee River and wind through hardwoods, pinelands, along ponds and cypress strands. Parts of the trek go off and on forest roads, but the Florida Trail remains well marked throughout the stimulating and wide-ranging terrain. The last part of the hike takes you over rolling pine/wiregrass hills to reach Concession Stand Camp, a fine overnight destination. Along the way you will pass another desirable backpack site.

---

**Distance & Configuration**: 15.0-mile there-and-back

**Difficulty**: Easy-moderate

**Outstanding Features**: Varied terrain, good designated campsites

**Scenery**: 4

**Solitude**: 3

**Family-Friendly**: 3

**Canine-Friendly**: 4

**Fees/Permits**: Free, reservable permit required

**Best Season**: Late October through late April

**Maps**: Green Swamp Wilderness Preserve West Tract

**For More Info**: Southwest Florida Water Management District, Bartow Service Office, 170 Century Blvd, Bartow, FL 33830-7700, 863-534-1448, https://www.swfwmd.state.fl.us/

**Finding the Trailhead**: From exit 32 on I-4 near Lakeland, take US 98 north for 13.2 miles, then turn right onto FL 471 north. Follow FL 471 for 4.6 miles to reach the trailhead parking area on your left, just after bridging the Withlacoochee River. GPS trailhead coordinates: 28.314898, -82.056075

---

The greater Green Swamp is a large wildland where the headwaters of four major Florida rivers begin—the Withlacoochee, the Hillsborough, the

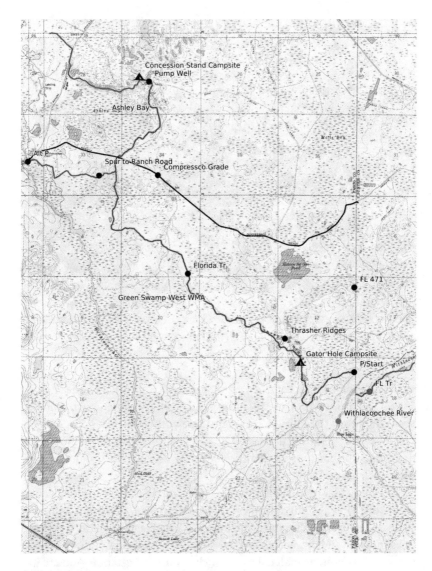

Ocklawaha, and the Peace. These waterways—and the swamp from which they came—are critical water supplies for the people, plants, and animals of Florida. Thus, the heart of the Green Swamp remains a protected place for nature to thrive and Florida's water table to replenish.

Luckily for us, a section of the fabled Florida Trail runs through the vast wildland, presenting varied scenery as well as designated campsites to which we can backpack. You must get a permit to overnight here, using the Southwest Florida Water Management District website. The trail itself is well marked and maintained, crossing a maze of forest and fire roads

Traipsing through a scrub oak dome on the fabled Florida Trail.

old and new. On the accompanying map, only Compressco Grade, a major forest road, is shown. Also, varied spur trails, some maintained by the Boy Scouts, spur off the Florida Trail, but these paths, too, can be in dubious shape as well as lead you astray. My advice is this: ignore the Boy Scout trails, the old forest roads, and stick with the Florida Trail, and you won't get turned around.

This particular trek explores the Green Swamp West tract. The first campsite, Gator Hole, is only 1.4 miles from the trailhead, making it a popular and easy destination. Leaving from the FL 471 trailhead, sometimes referred to as the McNeil entrance, follow the single-track Florida Trail westerly in pines with scattered small oaks and thicker varied vegetation. You are initially following a fading, slightly elevated logging tram. Curve southwest, working around a cypress strand at 0.8 mile. Here, turn north into drier woods with turkey oaks and live oaks. At 1.2 miles, pass a small pond on your right, briefly joining a sand road before returning to a small promontory above a pond/canal chain to your right.

At 1.4 miles, come to the Gator Hole Campsite on your left. The fine camp is set in a wide flat shaded by smallish live oaks, with picnic tables, fire ring, and ample tent sites. Use this camp if you're getting a late start. Water can be had from an adjacent canal. From here, the Florida Trail curves west, first into scrub and then amid a small set of hills and ponds collectively known as Thrasher Hills, per official USGS quadrangle maps.

Stay with the Florida Trail, going on and off old forest roads, avoiding mucky wetlands. At 3.1 miles, bridge a wet strand via culvert; then bridge a canal on a hiker bridge at 3.5 miles. Ahead, cross a palmetto prairie, then join a long straightaway bordered in pines. The landscape continues to change quickly, from live oaks to pines to open wetlands.

At 5.5 miles, bridge a small creek bordered in cypress. At 5.7 miles, reach a signed, legitimate trail intersection. Here, a blue-blazed spur goes left 1.5 miles to Ranch Road and alternate parking, near the Withlacoochee River. We stay straight with the Florida Trail, and its legendary orange blazes, soon crossing Compressco Grade, a well-maintained, unmistakable permanent forest road. Bridge a little wet branch on a hiker bridge, then weave through fast-changing forest scenery, including sandy scrub, pines, and turkey oaks amid some hills, with boggy Ashley Bay to your left.

At 6.5 miles, weave through wiregrass and pine hills. At 7.3 miles, cross a couple of forest roads, then curve west. Look left for a pump well after crossing the second forest road here. Beyond here, the Florida Trail angles along a hill, dropping to a cypress-bordered pond—another potential water source—to your right. At 7.5 miles, top a hill and reach an intersection. Here, a spur drops right to the intriguingly named Concession Stand Campsite, set in a flat among hills and ponds, shaded by some live oaks as well as scrub vegetation. The camp offers picnic table, fire ring, and tent sites. Last time I overnighted here the pump well was defunct. This campsite presents solitude and good varied scenery. After spending the night here, you can backtrack to the trailhead. For a longer trip, continue on the Florida Trail to Foster Bridge Campsite 2.6 miles beyond from Concession Stand Campsite, or High Bluff Campsite 5.3 miles past Foster Bridge Campsite.

## Mileages

- 0.0   FL 471 trailhead
- 1.4   Gator Hole Campsite
- 5.7   Spur goes left to Ranch Road
- 7.5   Short spur right to Concession Stand Campsite
- 15.0  FL 471 trailhead

# 27

## Tosohatchee Backpack

### Overview

This fine backpack winds amid low and lovely Tosohatchee WMA, where gorgeous live oak/palm/pine hammocks shade much of the route that uses a combination of the Florida Trail and other WMA hiking paths to make a circuit. Leave the park office on a white-blazed trail through mixed woods to meet the Florida Trail. Next traverse deep woods—palms and live oaks—exuding the real Florida. Turn south, tramping into a changing array of woodlands to reach Tiger Branch Campsite, set in pines and palms. From there, turn north, joining an old railroad grade before returning to the trailhead.

**Distance & Configuration**: 14.9-mile loop
**Difficulty**: Moderate
**Outstanding Features**: Palm/live oak hammocks, variety of ecosystems
**Scenery**: 5
**Solitude**: 3
**Family-Friendly**: 2
**Canine-Friendly**: 3
**Fees/permits**: Daily parking permit required
**Best Season**: Mid-December through mid-April
**Maps**: Tosohatchee WMA Brochure Map
**For More Info**: Tosohatchee WMA, 3365 Taylor Creek Rd, Christmas, FL 32709, 407-568-5893, https://myfwc.com/
**Finding the Trailhead**: From exit 215 on I-95 south of Titusville, take FL 50 west for 9.9 miles to turn left on Taylor Creek Road. Follow FL 50 for 2.9 miles to turn left into the WMA and Beehead Road. Follow it past the office on the left for a total of 0.5 mile to Parking Area 1 on the left. GPS trailhead coordinates: 28.498452, -80.996243

Make a loop backpack incorporating a stretch of the Florida Trail that runs through this eye-pleasing tract of land in the upper St. Johns River

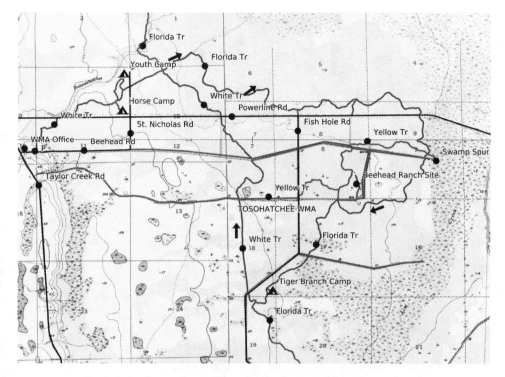

watershed. A cattle ranch a century back, the parcel later became a private hunting preserve before falling into the hands of the Florida Fish and Wildlife Commission. Tosohatchee offers multi-use activities from hunting to hiking, including backpacking. A designated backcountry campsite—Tiger Branch—is situated along this recommended one-night circuit backpack and makes for a fine camping experience. Mostly open and grassy amid scattered pines and palms, the campsite features two raised wooden tent platforms (the ground can be wet here), picnic tables, benches, and a fire ring, as well as a pitcher pump serving sulfurous water. You can cache water partway in the hike if you choose. Also, check hunt seasons before coming here, and wear orange if needed.

Tosohatchee is known as a wet place, so wait until at least mid-December for it to dry out before tackling this loop. Even so, the low live oak/palm hammocks may have mucky sections, but a nimble backpacker can stay dry shod. The trails combine mostly single-track with some double-tracks, and are well blazed. Stay with the blazes at all times, as the route splits off and on old woods roads.

The adventure starts a little beyond the park office at Parking Area 1. From there, walk just a few feet east on Beehead Road and then split left, joining the White Trail as it heads north as a double-track. At 0.3 mile, the

Palm cathedrals like this make Florida backpacking unique.

White Trail abruptly splits right as a single-track through brush with scattered pines. At 0.5 mile, emerge onto Powerline Road and follow it right, easterly, for 0.2 mile; then split left, north from the road. Watch the blazes carefully, as shortly the trail reenters palmetto prairie with scattered pines as a single-track path. Reenter woods of oak, pine, and palm, allowing a little more shade.

At 1.2 miles, a signed spur goes right toward the preserve horse camp. Ahead, a pair of blazed trails splits left for the preserve youth camp. Cross St. Nichols Road and a parking area at 1.4 miles. The path angles northeast on double-track to meet the Florida Trail at 1.9 miles. Here, begin the loop portion of the backpack. Stay straight on the Florida Trail, southbound, but heading northeast, still on double-track. At 2.3 miles, the Florida Trail abruptly splits right as a single-track, entering a pine/live oak/palm hammock. The woods form a shady roof, making it seem in the middle of nowhere—or just the right spot for a Florida backpacker. The everywhere-you-look beauty continues. Lower areas will include cypress and are the potentially muckiest locales.

At 4.0 miles, a blue-blazed trail leads right, south, to Fish Hole Road. A second spur leads to Powerline Road. Continue easterly in oak/palm hammock woods to pop out on Powerline Road at 5.7 miles. This could be a good place to cache water. Cross the road and a bridge a canal, reentering the palm/live oak hammock woods on the edge of a vast cypress swamp bordering the St. Johns River. At 6.3 miles, the Swamp Spur Trail leads left to the swamp's edge and the Yellow Trail goes right. Stay straight with the Florida Trail, heading south. Note the cedars hereabouts. Conditions become a little drier and piney as you come near the historic Beehead Ranch site. Ahead, cross low drainage ditches from the ranch days.

At 7.9 miles, reach a trail junction. Here, a spur goes right for Ranch Road. We stay left with the Florida Trail, and at 8.7 miles the wide Flowing Well Trail leaves right for Fish Hole Road. Stay straight with the Florida Trail, entering a low, moist area with scattered palms, pines and ferns. At 9.3 miles, the signed spur trail leads left 100 yards to the Tiger Branch Campsite. You can call the preserve office to reserve the site, no fee. The lights of Orlando to the northwest and Titusville to the east glow at night.

After overnighting here, rejoin the Florida Trail southbound, meeting the White Trail at 9.7 miles. Head right here on the White Trail, turning north toward the trailhead. Cross Fish Hole Road at 9.9 miles, then enter mixed woods, drier terrain, with lots of live oaks. Soon join an old former railroad logging grade, heading almost due north. The elevated berm makes for drier walking, but the narrow track line is partly grown over with trees, leaving you to dodge around them.

Nevertheless, the walking is easier, and you meet the other end of the Yellow Trail at 10.9 miles. Here, stay straight, soon leaving the old grade in thicker woods to bridge a canal; then cross gated Beehead Road at 11.7 miles. Keep northwesterly in pines to cross Powerline Road at a parking area at 12.3 miles. Stay northwesterly, back in those gorgeous palm/live oak hammock woods. Hike through this highlight of the Tosohatchee one more time before completing the loop portion of the hike at 13.0 miles. From here it is a backtrack to the trailhead, completing the adventure at 14.9 miles.

## Mileages

| | |
|---|---|
| 0.0 | Parking Area 1 |
| 1.9 | Join Florida Trail |
| 5.7 | Cross Powerline Road |
| 9.3 | Spur to Tiger Branch Camp |
| 12.3 | Cross Powerline Road |
| 14.9 | Parking Area 1 |

# 28

## Bull Creek Backpack

### Overview

Superior scenery makes this loop backpack a winner. Known for its palmetto and wiregrass prairies with distant views, this circuit also leads you past cypress domes, sand pine scrub, and along Bull Creek using a historic railroad grade. Generally done as a long one-nighter, this trek can easily be stretched to two nights.

---

**Distance & Configuration**: 17.5-mile loop

**Difficulty**: Moderate, does have open, sunny stretches

**Outstanding Features**: Distant views, varied habitats, historic railroad grade

**Scenery**: 5

**Solitude**: 3

**Family-Friendly**: 2

**Canine-Friendly**: 3

**Fees/Permits**: None required

**Best Season**: Late October through March

**Maps**: Herky Huffman/Bull Creek Wildlife Management Area (WMA)

**For More Info**: Bull Creek WMA, FWC Northeast Region, Northeast Region, 1239 SW 10th St, Ocala, FL 34471-0323, 352-732-1225, https://myfwc.com/

**Finding the Trailhead**: From exit 180 on I-95 west of Melbourne, take US 192 west for 19.2 miles to turn left onto Crabgrass Road. Follow it for 6 miles as it heads southeasterly to enter Bull Creek WMA. The backpack starts at the campground entrance to the right, just before reaching the wildlife check station. GPS trailhead coordinates: 28.083101, -80.962788

---

Bull Creek WMA is a Florida gem, preserving a mosaic of scenic habitats. A segment of the Florida Trail runs through the preserve, and connector trails allow you to make a worthy loop. Little Scrub designated camp is set partway on the route. The sandy site is located in low scrub oaks, limiting

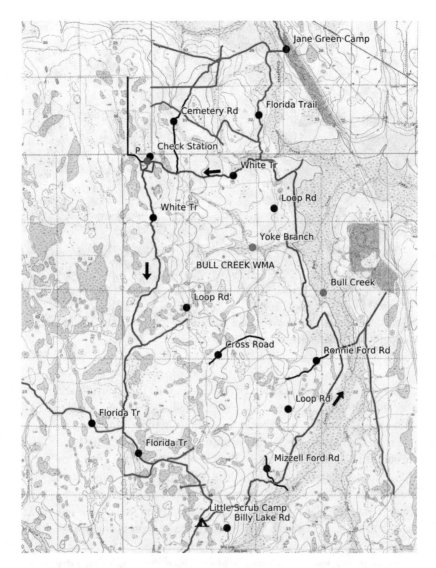

shade, but it does have a fire ring, picnic tables, benches, a pump well, and ample tent sites.

Much of the backpack's first half is open to the sun, traversing the palmetto prairies from which rise domes of cypress scattered on the horizon. The second half runs roughly parallel to Bull Creek in generally thicker woods. You can turn this one-night loop into a two-night adventure by taking the Florida Trail north 2.1 miles to the Jane Green backcountry campsite, then backtracking to the main loop, adding 4.2 miles to the trip.

Part of this backpack traces an old railroad grade.

As with other backpacking destinations in state forests, national forests, and wildlife management areas, check ahead about hunting seasons and plan to wear blaze orange if backpacking during those times.

From the hunter check station, head south, following the White Trail through the hunter's campground, scattered with trailers. At 0.1 mile, the trail enters wiregrass prairie with scattered pines. These wide-open spaces are pocked with small grassy ponds and also the aforementioned cypress domes. At 0.3 mile, pass the foundation of an old building to your left. At 0.8 mile, make your way across the wet outflow of a cypress dome, a creek per se, with attendant trees along its strand. At 1.3 miles, the White Trail winds between grassy ponds. The trails here are generally routed to the driest terrain. At 1.6 miles, cross another outflow of a cypress dome. Ahead rises big-sky country, where tawny wiregrass and green palmetto avail an open sweep of the land.

Bridge a grown-over canal by culvert at 2.7 miles. The path follows and crosses occasional double-tracks but is mostly single-track trail. These turns are blazed and clearly marked. At 4.6 miles, meet the Florida Trail beside a wire fence. Keep straight, heading south, joining the Florida Trail. Keep threading between wetter cypress domes on drier prairie of palmetto, blueberry, and fetterbush. Stay with the blazes as the Florida Trail goes off and on old roads under open sky. Many of the blazes are on posts.

At 6.6 miles, touch Billy Lake Road before turning south into sand pine scrub. This is a good place to cache water if you are staying at Little Scrub Campsite. Carefully stay with the orange blazes to reach Little Scrub Campsite at 7.0 miles. Beyond the campsite, the now-sandy Florida Trail continues through oak and sand pine scrub, crossing Billy Lake Road at 7.5 miles. Enter wiregrass/pine habitat. Observe the land sloping toward Bull Creek. Ahead, cross the first of many small wooded creek strands flowing toward Bull Creek, divided by palmetto and wiregrass prairie. Foot bridges offer passage over most creeks. At 8.3 miles, cross the gravel road leading to old Mizzell Ford.

Keep northeast in scattered palms, live oaks, and pines to join the old Union Cypress logging railroad grade at 8.9 miles. In operation from 1912 to 1932, this tram extracted cypress from Bull Creek and environs and then took it to Melbourne to be milled. A century later the cypress has returned in stature. The Florida Trail follows this railroad grade for several miles, occasionally detouring. The grade is partly grown over by trees but is generally drier ground. Hiker footbridges span creeks and canals.

The berm generally runs parallel to Bull Creek, with cypress to the right and pines and prairie to the left. In places the berm cuts through wet cypress swamps with water on both sides. Watch for cypress knees protruding from the trailbed in these spots. At 11.1 miles, the trail crosses Ronnie Ford Road. At 11.7 miles, turn away from the berm, going through scattered oaks. Rejoin the berm once more; then, at 13.3 miles, pop out on Loop Road and turn right, spanning Yoke Branch on the road bridge.

The Florida Trail turns right down Yoke Branch and then rejoins the logging grade at 13.7 miles. Travel almost due north in swampy woods with more hiker footbridges. At 14.5 miles, the Florida Trail leaves the grade for good and then joins a double-track southwest to pop out on Loop Road yet again at 14.9 miles. Here, stay with the Florida Trail as it turns north, opening onto more palmetto prairie, before turning west along a tributary of Crabgrass Creek. Reach a trail junction at 15.4 miles. Here, you can turn the one-night trip into a two-night trip by detouring on the Florida Trail 2.1 miles to Jane Green Campsite. It offers picnic table, fire ring, and a pump well, set in pine woods.

Our loop keeps west, now on the White Trail, running the margin betwixt the streamside woods to the right and prairie to the left. Cross a wooded creek strand at 16.1 miles, opening onto pine-studded prairie once again, soaking in those distant views a final time. Emerge at Cemetery Road at 17.0

miles. Here, walk a few feet and then keep west on Loop Road, tracing it for a half mile to the hunter's check station and backpack's end at 17.5 miles.

## Mileages

- 0.0   Hunter's campground/check station
- 4.6   Join Florida Trail
- 7.0   Little Scrub Campsite
- 8.9   Join old Union Cypress logging railroad grade
- 13.3  Bridge Yoke Branch on Loop Road
- 15.4  Join White Trail (Florida Trail heads north 2.1 miles to Jane Green Campsite)
- 17.5  Hunter's campground/check station

# 29

## Three Lakes Backpack

### Overview

Make a figure-eight loop on this backpack, traversing miles of gorgeous live oak hammocks as well as pine flatwoods and beside wooded creeks at Three Lakes Wildlife Management Area (WMA). Follow the Florida Trail, crossing a stream strand, and then enter oak hammocks. Join the Three Lakes Loop, detouring to an exquisite view of Lake Marian. Hike through more hammocks to rejoin the Florida Trail, nearing Lake Jackson, reaching isolated Dry Pond Campsite. Complete the lower loop and then come by shady Parker Hammock Campsite. Travel the margin between pretty Parker Slough and open prairie before completing the second loop.

**Distance & Configuration**: 11.3-mile figure-eight loop

**Difficulty**: Moderate

**Outstanding Features**: Hardwood hammocks, lake views, good campsites

**Scenery**: 5

**Solitude**: 3

**Family-Friendly**: 4

**Canine-Friendly**: 4

**Fees/Permits**: Day-use permit required; free camping permit required

**Best Season**: November through mid-April

**Maps**: Three Lakes WMA—Prairie Lakes Unit Recreation Guide

**For more info**: Florida Fish and Wildlife Conservation Commission, Northeast Region, 1239 SW 10th St, Ocala, FL 34471, 352-732-1225, https://myfwc.com/

**Finding the Trailhead**: From the intersection of US 441 and FL 60 at Yeehaw Junction west of Vero Beach, take US 441 north for 14.1 miles. Then turn left onto Canoe Creek Road and follow it for 9.5 miles, turning left into Three Lakes WMA, Prairie Lakes Unit, and following Prairie Lakes Road for 0.1 mile to parking area on your right. GPS trailhead coordinates: 27.927602, -81.124900

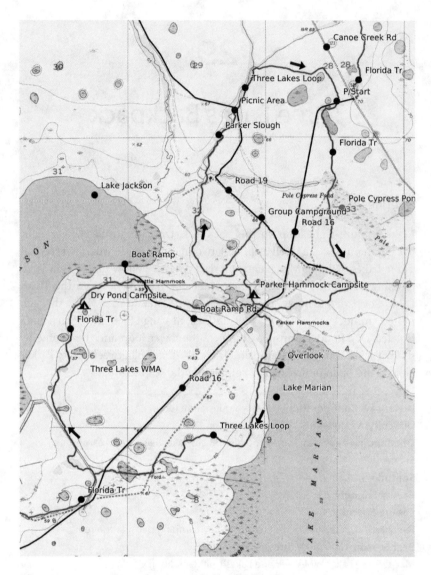

The attractive Prairie Lakes Unit of Three Lakes WMA is the setting for this eye-pleasing overnighter combining the Florida Trail with additional trails that allow for a double loop traveling miles of live oak hammocks. Expect loads of superior scenery, and you will not be disappointed. You can reverse the loops or do them individually. Before heading out, make sure to call to reserve your campsite—though free, the sites must be reserved ahead of time. Also, pay attention to hunt dates on the tract; backpacking is not allowed during hunt dates. Finally, when arriving, pay your day-use fee at the parking area kiosk.

Three Lakes WMA is known for its distant prairie vistas.

After getting your ducks in a row, begin backpacking this slice of preserved Central Florida. Your first habitat is pine flatwoods, as you join the single-track Florida Trail, skirting a cypress swamp as the path heads southbound, with prairie off to your right. At 0.6 mile, come to the Pole Cypress Ponds. Take the 0.1-mile-long boardwalk through the wooded wetland, passing an elevated observation bench before returning to ground and scattered evergreens. Enter an oak hammock, passing within sight of the WMA offices before passing under a power line at 1.5 miles; then enter a gorgeous live oak hammock with widespread arms towering over a minimal understory. Pass a water control structure before popping out on Road 16 at 2.3 miles. Turn left on the road to cross a canal.

At 2.4 miles, split left back into woods, now following the white-blazed Three Lakes Loop, traversing a pine palm hammock. Enjoy the hammock hiking on a dappled forest floor, where resurrection ferns and epiphytes thrive on the live oaks above. At 2.8 miles, take the spur trail left to the Lake Marian Overlook, tracing an old elevated road east, reaching the viewpoint at 3.0 miles. Gaze out on the 5,700-acre expansive body of water stretching east to the horizon.

Resume the Three Lakes Loop, heading southwest, mostly in live oak/palm hammocks, occasionally opening to prairie views, crossing an old ditch by 3.8 miles. At 4.6 miles, bridge a more substantial canal. Turn west, still in woods, crossing Road 16 to reunite with the Florida Trail at 5.1 miles. You are northbound now, in palms and live oaks. In spots, the tree cover thins. Cross the bigger canal a second time at 5.5 miles. At 6.7 miles, come to the short spur right to Dry Pond Campsite, equipped with picnic table, fire ring, and pump well. A view opens east from the live oak–shaded camp.

Continuing the backpack, keep north in live oaks to reach an auto-turn-around and auto-camping area off Boat Ramp Road at 7.1 miles. Shortly cross Boat Ramp Road, now eastbound in woods. Bridge a major canal at 8.2 miles and then reach a trail intersection. Here, stay left, once again on the Three Lakes Loop, as the Florida Trail goes right to quickly reach Road 16. At 8.3 miles, come to Parker Hammock Campsite, set on a short spur. It offers multiple sites with picnic tables, fire ring, an upright grill, pump well, and a wooden tent platform. At 8.7 miles, a spur trail leads right to the WMA's group campground.

Stay with the Three Lakes Loop, coming along forest-encased Parker Slough at 9.5 miles, bridging a tributary of the slough ahead. Continue along the margin of prairie and forest to emerge at a picnic area to cross Road 10 at 10.0 miles. Stay along the edge of the slough before turning away to open terrain, passing a small pond before completing the scenic loop at 11.3 miles.

## Mileages

0.0  Canoe Creek Road trailhead
2.4  Join Three Lakes Loop
3.0  Lake Marian Overlook
5.1  Rejoin Florida Trail
6.7  Dry Pond Campsite
7.1  Cross Boat Ramp Road
8.3  Parker Hammock Campsite
11.3  Canoe Creek Road trailhead

### Trip Planning Is an Important Component of Backpacking

I have a backpacking friend in Central Florida. I was eager to backpack a section of the Florida Trail, the long-distance path slated to run from the Big Cypress to Gulf Islands National Seashore. My Central Florida friend advised me to pick a section of trail I wanted to hike, and he would ac-commodate the request. I picked a 67-mile segment through the Ocala National Forest.

The two of us took off. That night around the campfire, I mentioned our nearly ideal backpacking progress, averaging 11 miles per day through the sand pine scrub. This pace would lead us to our desired endpoint when the five-night trip was over.

That was when my buddy mentioned that this was a three-night trip and he had to be at work on the fourth day. A simple misunderstanding of dates had led to this dilemma. So what once was a casual backpacking trip became a hike-athon.

We pushed hard those last two days, marking mileage, hiking hour after hour. It was painful to pass so much beauty without giving the Florida Trail the attention it deserved.

Don't let this happen to you.

Before you start a backpacking adventure, get together with fellow members of your party to plan your trip. Go over the practicalities of the trip—who, what, where, when, and how. You also need to go over gear, especially gear to be shared by the group, whether it is the tents, cooking items, and the like. Also go over the transportation and parking situations.

When getting a backcountry group together, consider the following things: group size, group dynamics, and trip expectations. The more people in a party, the more complicated things become.

For backpackers, I suggest keeping your group small, as this offers the best camping opportunities. You may not want to mix your hard-partying college classmate with the deacon at church. I prefer to keep backpacking groups no bigger than four people. Having too many people requires too large a campsite (not always easy to find) as well as increasing the impact a single group can have on a camp.

Trip expectations are very important. Everyone needs to be on the same wavelength as to what the trip will be like. For example, does everyone want to hike hard all day long and spend very little time at camp? Or do they want to spend more time telling backpacking tales by the fire than actually backpacking? Is everyone willing to go for all five nights, or will someone want to leave early? Make sure everyone agrees about the length and style of the trip.

Also, make it clear up front about sharing expenses, chores, and other duties. This way there will be no unpleasant surprises when it comes time to collect money—or firewood. Even after all parties come to agreement about the adventure, review the details one last time. That way you won't end up hiking too far in too short a period—like I did—because of a simple misunderstanding.

# 30

## Lake Wales Ridge Backpack

### Overview

This loop backpack—one of my favorites—has it all. Great campsites and gorgeous varied scenery and good trails add up to a first-rate Florida backpack experience at Lake Wales Ridge State Forest. First, cruise bluffs above comely Reedy Creek; then make your way to alluring Lake Arbuckle. Trek its shores and then explore sand pine scrub and pine flatwoods before coming along Grassy Creek. Close the loop hiking bluffs above Livingston Creek and Reedy Creek. Along the way you can camp at any of five reservable campsites that match the high standards of the scenery at this state forest.

**Distance & Configuration**: 20.1-mile loop with spurs
**Difficulty**: Moderate–difficult
**Outstanding Features**: Scenery, reservable campsites, backwoods streams
**Scenery**: 5
**Solitude**: 2
**Family-Friendly**: 3
**Canine-Friendly**: 3
**Fees/permits**: Fee campsites
**Best Season**: November through mid-April
**Maps**: Lake Wales Ridge State Forest
**For More Info**: Lake Wales Ridge State Forest, 851 CR 630 E, Frostproof, FL 33843, 863-589-0545, https://www.fdacs.gov/, Campsite reservations: https://www.reserveamerica.com/
**Finding the Trailhead**: From the intersection of US 98/US 27 and FL 17 in Avon Park just south of Frostproof, take FL 17 north for 3.5 miles. Then turn right on Wilson Road and follow it east for 2 miles, keeping straight as the road changes to Lake Reedy Boulevard. Continue for 1.5 more miles and then turn right onto Lake Arbuckle Road, following it for 1.5 miles to turn right onto Rucks Dairy Road. Keep south for 0.8 mile, reaching the trailhead parking area on

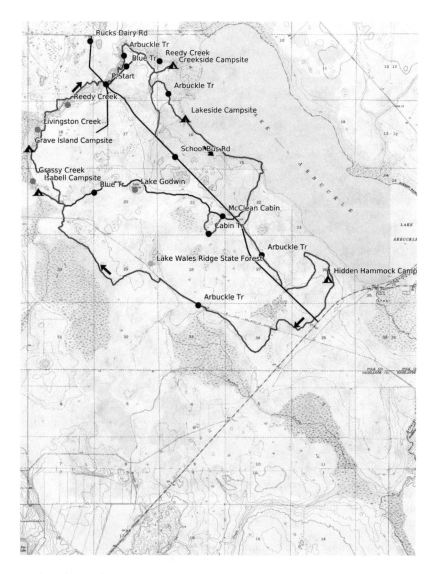

the left just after bridging Reedy Creek. GPS trailhead coordinates: 27.708202, -81.446006

---

Lake Wales Ridge State Forest harbors a treasure trove of rare and imperiled flora and fauna. Not only can we rejoice in this parcel of Florida being preserved, but we can explore its many ecosystems, including nearly gone locales where cutthroat grass seeps are topped with slash pines, among other ecosystems. Wildlife is abundant, with bear, deer, and wild turkey traipsing

Backpack along bluffs overlooking Reedy Creek.

the forest. I enjoy traveling along the streams of the forest—Reedy Creek, Grassy Creek, and Livingston Creek.

And for backpackers like us, the ideal reservable campsites cap the adventure. Make sure to reserve your chosen sites well ahead of time on winter weekends. Start the backpack by leaving south from the trailhead, walking along sand School Bus Road. After a short distance, the yellow-blazed Arbuckle Trail splits left into sand pine scrub woods. Just ahead, a blue-blazed alternate path beelines northeast. Stay with the Arbuckle Trail and shortly come alongside Reedy Creek. Cruise bluffs above the tea-colored stream, bending with the curves of the waterway. Good looks open on creek bends, where lush hammock vegetation below contrasts with scrub on the bluff.

Revel in this section before pulling away from the stream. At 1.7 miles, reach the spur trail to Creekside Campsite. Trace the wide track through hammock woods to reach the first-rate camp at 2.0 miles. Perched along the banks of Reedy Creek under a cathedral-esque canopy of live oaks, the recommended campsite is complemented with a picnic table and fire ring. Get your water from Reedy Creek.

Resume the loop, entering slash pine woods rising above palmetto and rosemary. Stay with the yellow blazes as the route goes off and on double-track. At 2.6 miles, near thick woods, a blazed spur leads right to School Bus Road. Stay left with the Arbuckle Trail. Watch out for unlabeled fire lanes. The woods thicken as you come closer to Lake Arbuckle. At 3.5 miles, bridge a trickling branch twice in succession, reaching Lakeside Campsite at 3.6 miles. The camp is set where live oaks meld with shoreline cypress. A layer of grassy weeds tops the lake, preventing aquatic access here. Get your water from the stream just crossed. The setting is fine with water views and breezes swaying the heavy growth of Spanish moss in the trees.

The next part of the trek is superlatively scenic as you hike south along the shore of the lake, passing sporadic small beaches, from which rise cypress behind which rise live oak/pine/palm hammocks, the whole of which is more than worthy of preservation. Watch for cypress knees rising from the trailbed. Bridge occasional seasonal creeks flowing into Lake Arbuckle. At 4.6 miles, pass a sand road leading right, up and away from the water. At 5.3 miles, turn away from the lake and rise into a changed landscape of sandy oak and pine scrub. Note the hills here. At 5.9 miles, a blue-blazed trail splits right toward the McClean Cabin and splits the greater backpack loop in half.

We're going the whole way, and stay left, coming near School Bus Road at 6.2 miles. Here, a short spur leads right to the road. We head southeast in scrubby woods to pop out on School Bus Road at 7.4 miles, using the road to span a small stream by culvert. Reenter forest, working through pine flatwoods. Come near Lake Arbuckle and run the margin between pines and lush woods. At 8.8 miles, now in scrub, a spur leads right 0.2 mile to Hidden Hammock Campsite, set in an oak hammock, regenerating from a past burn. There is no water here. Either cache water on School Bus Road or get it at the 7.4-mile mark.

Return to the Arbuckle Trail, traveling through sandy oak scrub, scattered with sand pine and lichens in places. At 10.1 miles, cross School Bus Road. The Arbuckle Trail works through pines. Curve back north, making the loop. The trail goes on and off sand roads, varying between single-track and double-track. At 10.9 miles, cross elevated Tram Road, closed to public motor use. Curve northwest. At 12.1 miles, hike through pine/cutthroat grass seeps. Reach and join Tram Road at 12.5 miles. Keep on the elevated road with a tributary of Bonnet Creek to your left, surrounded by impenetrable hammock/swamp vegetation.

At 13.4 miles, leave left from Tram Road, entering pine flatwoods to reach the margin of a big wooded swamp, rich with bay trees. Turn right, north here, traveling the margin between the wooded swamp to the left, with scrub and pines to the right. Continue on and off fire roads. Stay with the blazes. At 15.7 miles, bridge a canal after passing through a wooded copse with resting bench. At 16.0 miles, the major blue-blazed trail shortcutting the greater loop comes in. Stay left here, and at 16.1 miles, split left on the spur to highly recommended Isabell Campsite, reached at 16.4 miles. The camp, with standard fire ring and picnic table, stands under live oaks and pines next to swift and scenic Grassy Creek.

To continue the loop, backtrack to the Arbuckle Trail, heading north in mixed woods, parallel to Grassy Creek to reach the spur to Grave Island Campsite at 17.9 miles. Head left here, westerly, to bridge Livingston Creek (Grassy Creek is a tributary of Livingston Creek) and reach smaller Grave Island Campsite, set in scrub oaks and smaller live oaks, overlooking Livingston Creek. It is a little more used than Isabell Campsite. Backtrack, continuing north to span Reedy Creek on a sturdy trail bridge at 18.7 miles. Follow Reedy Creek downstream on sand and oak scrub bluffs, as well as a fence line, working around an inholding. Stay on the creek contours, with lush riparian woods to your right and scrub to your left. Pop out on Rucks Dairy Road and turn right, bridging Reedy Creek on the road to return to the trailhead, completing the first-rate backpack at 20.1 miles.

## Mileages

| | |
|---|---|
| 0.0 | Trailhead |
| 2.0 | Creekside Campsite |
| 3.6 | Lakeside Campsite |
| 5.9 | Blue-blazed cross trail |
| 7.4 | Pop out on School Bus Road |
| 9.0 | Hidden Hammock Campsite |
| 10.1 | Cross School Bus Road |
| 16.0 | Other end of blue-blazed cross trail |
| 16.4 | Isabell Campsite |
| 17.9 | Grave Island Campsite |
| 20.1 | Trailhead |

# 31

# Kissimmee Prairie Backpack

## Overview

Soak in the famed dark sky while overnighting here at big Kissimmee Prairie Preserve State Park, a certified dark sky park. For a good one-night family trip, head across some of the restored prairie to appreciate big sky by day to reach a fine live oak hammock, where you will camp. That night, soak in the starry skies from adjacent grassland. Next day, loop back to the trailhead.

**Distance & Configuration**: 4.6-mile loop
**Difficulty**: Easy
**Outstanding Features**: Certified dark sky park, great campsite, big views
**Scenery**: 4
**Solitude**: 3
**Family-Friendly**: 5
**Canine-Friendly**: 4
**Fees/Permits**: Fee campsite
**Best Season**: November through mid-April
**Maps**: Kissimmee Prairie Preserve State Park Trail Map & Guide
**For More Info**: Kissimmee Prairie Preserve State Park, 33104 NW 192nd Ave, Okeechobee, FL 34972, 863-462-5360, https://www.floridastateparks.org/
**Finding the Trailhead**: From the intersection of US 441 and FL 60 at Yeehaw Junction west of Vero Beach, take US 441 south for 17.7 miles. Then turn right on NW 240th Street and follow it for 13.2 miles to turn right onto NW 192 Ave/ Peavine Trail. Follow it 5.1 miles to enter Kissimmee Prairie Preserve State Park. Continue in the park for 4.8 more miles and then turn left, heading west for 1.8 miles to reach the park office on your left, where you obtain your camping permit. From there, continue west and then turn into the equestrian campground, where you will find the Prairie Loop trailhead. GPS trailhead coordinates: 27.583509, -81.051737

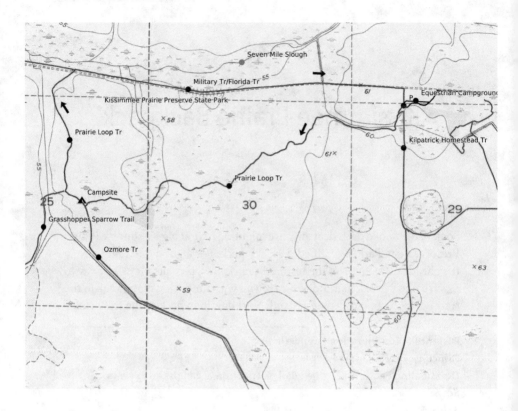

Located in Okeechobee County east of the Kissimmee River, Kissimmee Prairie Preserve covers a whopping 54,000 acres far removed from the glowing urbanity of Florida that helps qualify the state park as an official dark sky park, where you can view not only a blanket of stars but also launches from space centers on Florida's east coast. And in addition to the immense star-viewing opportunities at Kissimmee Prairie Preserve, you will also find smaller wonders, from gopher frogs to rare butterflies to the crested caracara. Black bears and Florida panthers are known to pass through this big preserve of vast dry prairies, wooded sloughs, and hardwood hammocks such as the one where a fine backcountry campsite is located.

The backcountry campsite contains three individual camps. One site offers an open-sided shelter picnic table and fire ring. Another is housed on the east side of the hammock shaded by a big live oak, with fire ring and picnic table. The third site offers the most solitude and is virtually encircled by shady live oaks. A fine pump well serves the greater camp. Call the park office for backcountry campsite reservations.

Kissimmee Prairie is Florida's "Big Sky Country."

From the west end of the equestrian campground, take the Prairie Loop Trail, heading west on double-track along a thin strip of oaks and palms, festooned with ferns, epiphytes, and Spanish moss. At 0.1 mile, bridge a shallow canal and reach an intersection. Here, the Kilpatrick Homestead Trail goes left, but we stay right, still westbound along the tree line, sometimes in the trees and sometimes along the prairie edge, presenting southward vistas to palm and oak islands in the sea of grasses and palmetto, as well as low-lying seasonal wetlands.

At 0.9 mile, pop out in wide-open prairie. The trail's westerly wanderings may seem random, but the path is working around seasonal wetlands. At 1.7 miles, enter a cool, dark hammock, popping out after 0.1 mile. At 2.1 miles, reach an intersection. Here the Ozmore Trail splits left, but we turn right, entering another hammock and the backcountry camping area. Just ahead is the pump well, and Campsite 1, with the shelter, to the left. Campsite 2 is around the corner and well shaded by live oaks. Campsite 3 is well shaded and offers maximum solitude. This is a good place to overnight. After setting up camp, make plans as to exactly where you will go to view the night sky, as the live oak/palm hammock is encircled by prairie. Consider bringing binoculars to enhance your star viewing at this certified dark sky park.

Your return trip will bring more views of prairie, tree islands, and seasonal wetlands. Continue west through the camping hammock, passing the Grasshopper Sparrow Trail and then turning north into open prairie. At 2.4 miles, come along a line of trees to your left but stay in open country. At 2.9 miles, reach an old east-west elevated road-turned-path, Military Trail. Here, the Florida Trail runs in conjunction with Military Trail. Head east on Military Trail/Florida Trail. Brushy Seven Mile Slough flows to your left. Over time, the hydrology of the park is being restored from dug canals draining former pasture to natural wetlands. So far more than 70 miles of canals and ditches have been restored. Park lands stretch out in all directions—willow thickets, brush marshes, glassy prairie, hardwood tree islands. The walking is easy, allowing long looks, absorbing distant views many people believe can't be had in the Sunshine State. At 4.5 miles, split right toward the equestrian campground, and you are back at the trailhead, completing the dark-sky park backpack at 4.6 miles.

## Mileages

0.0   Prairie Loop trailhead
2.1   Backcountry campground
2.9   Right on Military Trail/Florida Trail
4.6   Prairie Loop trailhead

# 32

~~~~~~~~~~~~~~

# Saint Sebastian Backpack

## Overview

Enjoy this great family overnighter at one of Florida's newer state parks. Hike through preserved sand scrub, pine woods, and limited wetlands to reach the lush forest on bluffs of the Saint Sebastian River, where you can overnight it at Mullet Camp. Your return trip takes advantage of additional trails to create a loop back to the trailhead.

**Distance & Configuration**: 5.4-mile balloon loop
**Difficulty**: Easy
**Outstanding Features**: Quality riverside campsite
**Scenery**: 4
**Solitude**: 2
**Family-Friendly**: 5
**Canine-Friendly**: 4
**Fees/Permits**: Fee campsite
**Best Season**: November through mid-April
**Maps**: Saint Sebastian River Preserve State Park
**For More Info**: Saint Sebastian River Preserve State Park, 1000 Buffer Preserve Dr, Fellsmere, Florida 32948, 321-953-5005, https://www.floridastateparks.org/
**Finding the Trailhead**: From exit 156 on I-95 near the town of Sebastian, take CR 512 east for 1.9 miles to turn left on Ranch Road. Follow it 1.3 miles to a parking area on your left, across the road from the park picnic area, on the right. The actual hike starts on the right about 100 yards north on Ranch Road. GPS trailhead coordinates: 27.784653, -80.527636

Saint Sebastian Preserve State Park protects 22,000 acres of wildland near the coastal community of Sebastian, just north of Vero Beach. Even though civilization creeps up to the park's boundaries, the destination is a pleasing place to backpack. Broken into four separate but adjacent tracts, the preserve offers a total of nine fee-based, reservable backcountry campsites

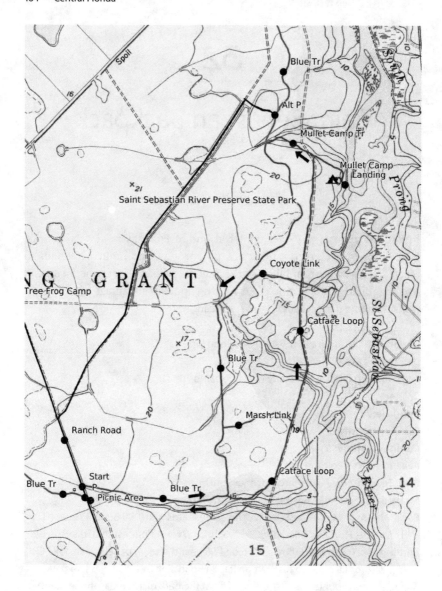

among the four parcels, shared with equestrians and bicycle campers. Call the park to reserve your site. Most of the trails are open double-tracks. Bring a sun hat and sunscreen.

Our overnighter takes place in the southeast quadrant of the park. Here, the Blue Trail makes a big loop, and we use that trail to leave east from the trailhead, after walking north on Ranch Road from the picnic parking area. From the road, head east on the Blue Trail, a gated grassy double-track. Quickly pass under a power line. Pine, palms, and oaks border the trail.

Your campsite here is just back from the Saint Sebastian River.

Keep an eye peeled for abundant deer. At 0.6 mile, reach the loop portion of the hike. Stay right easterly, on the Catface Loop. Be watchful as unsigned sand fire roads spur off the main trail. Blazes and arrows keep you on the correct route. The terrain becomes less vegetated and the trail sandier as you head north. The thick line of vegetation to your right is the Saint Sebastian River. At 1.1 miles, the Marsh Link goes left, but we stay straight on the

Catface Loop, in mostly open terrain. At 1.3 miles, bridge a tributary of the Saint Sebastian River in dense vegetation.

At 1.7 miles, the Coyote Link Trail goes left and right, but we stay straight with the Catface Loop in open lands dotted with a few pines, reaching the Mullet Camp Trail at 2.3 miles. Head right here on a sandy double-track, easterly. Noticeably descend toward the Saint Sebastian River, entering heavier woods of live oaks, palm, and pine.

At 2.5 miles, you enter a clearing, centered with what remains of an old coquina block foundation. The river is to your left, below a substantial bluff, complemented by a shaded picnic table. Stairs lead down to a canoe/kayak landing. We turn right near the foundation to enter recommended Mullet Camp, a cleared area bordered in palms and pine, and complemented with a fire ring, sitting benches, and picnic table, as well as tent sites. Remember, bring your own water. Also, reservations are required. Mullet Camp can be popular, since it is accessible from the water as well as land.

After overnighting in this riverside spot, backtrack, looping back to the trailhead via the Blue Loop. Continue west beyond the Catface Loop to reach another intersection at 3.0 miles. To your right, a short trail goes to an alternate parking area. We go left, turning back south on the Blue Trail. Head through mixed vegetation, from pines to live oaks to brush, scattered in a lot of open flats. Work around some wetlands to your right before intersecting the other end of the Coyote Link at 3.8 miles. Keep straight, shortly bridging a canal to enter pine flatwoods. Stay with the blazes to pass the other end of the Marsh Link at 4.5 miles. Curve around a brushy pond and then, at 4.8 miles, complete the loop portion of the backpack. From here it is a simple 0.6 mile backtrack to the trailhead, finishing the backpack.

## Mileages

0.0  Trailhead
2.5  Mullet Camp
5.4  Trailhead

# South Florida

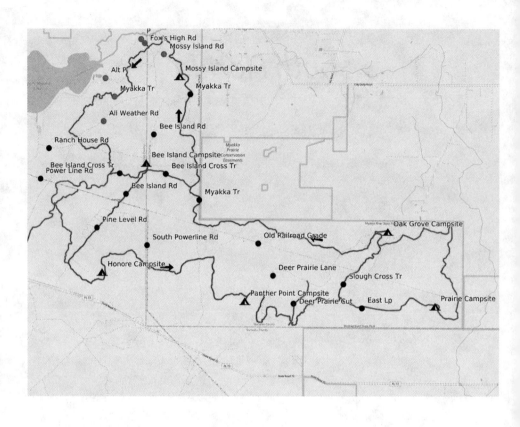

# 33

## Myakka River State Park Backpack

### Overview

Take the hiker-only Myakka Trail and some double-tracks to fashion a big exploratory loop at big Myakka River State Park. Dense palm islands, shady oak hammocks, and open grass/palmetto prairies present contrasting environments as you hike past several designated, reservable campsites. The open-prairie parts of the trek present distant views while the camps are set in shady hammocks.

**Distance & Configuration**: 29.2-mile loop
**Difficulty**: Difficult due to distance
**Outstanding Features**: Prairie views, varied environments, good campsites
**Scenery**: 5
**Solitude**: 2
**Family-Friendly**: 3
**Canine-Friendly**: 3
**Fees/Permits**: Fee backcountry permit required
**Best Season**: November through March
**Maps**: Myakka River State Park, Hiking & Biking Myakka River State Park
**For More Info**: Myakka River State Park, 13208 SR 72, Sarasota, FL 34241, 941-361-6511, https://www.floridastateparks.org/
**Finding the Trailhead**: From exit 205 on I-75 east in Sarasota, take FL 72 east for 8.8 miles to turn left into Myakka River State Park. Stay with the main park road for 5.9 miles to reach the gated entrance for Fox's High Road on your right. Park on the road shoulder and don't block the gate. GPS trailhead coordinates: 27.286032, -82.255053

Covering 58 square miles, Myakka River State Park delivers a big backcountry to explore. The Myakka Trail makes a 39-mile circuit, passing by six reservable designated backcountry campsites. Additionally, gated fire roads, open only to park personnel but doubling as hiker trails, crisscross the land

This backpack traverses open prairies and deep woods.

of open prairies, oak hammocks, and wooded wetlands, allowing you numerous backcountry adventure options, fashioning trips of two, three, or even four nights. Our loop travels by the only two backcountry campsites with working pump wells, Bee Island and Oak Grove. (At one time, all six sites had pump wells. The park needs to rectify this.) These pump wells don't have the tastiest water in the world, so bring drink mixes to mask the iron/sulfur taint. If you stay at any of the other sites, you need to bring your own water or get it from aboveground sources still holding aqua during the winter hiking season. (Don't come here in summer, the heat and bugs will run you out.) Although you can reserve campsites, multiple parties are allowed to stay at each site. Call the park office to reserve a site. Much of the hiking is done in open prairie. Be prepared for sun and wind—and some of the best views in Florida. You will cross occasional bridges spanning old canals or sloughs—potential water sources.

Fire is liberally used to keep the land in its natural state, home to burrowing owls, the grasshopper sparrow, and more than forty plant species per square yard. The prairies are dotted with grassy depression marshes. Deer Prairie Slough is a linear wooded wetland along which the Myakka Trail travels for miles. Though scenic, with its willows and cypresses, water is not easy to access. You will see wild pigs, or at least the damage they do to the land, digging up terrain while looking for food. They are an exotic threat to the native park flora and fauna.

The recommended backpack can be shortened or lengthened according to your desires. Upon arriving, get your permit and pay the modest camping fee at the park entrance station; then begin at the less-used Fox's High Road trailhead. Trace the sandy double-track southeast in a grove of palm and oak with a superstory of pine, meeting the single-track hiker-only Myakka Trail at 0.2 mile. Head right here, quickly opening onto prairie, then straddling the border between prairie and forest. At 1.1 miles, a hiking spur goes right to the Fox's Lower Road trailhead. We stay left, crossing Fox's Lower Road. At 1.5 miles, bridge a canal and then reenter forest ahead. Wind through woods, turning southeast to cross All Weather Road at 3.6 miles; then bridge a ditch and cross Ranch House Road. Cross Ranch House Road again at 4.1 and again at 4.5 miles, bridging a few canals along the way.

At 5.0 miles, temporarily leave the Myakka Trail left, joining single-track Bee Island Cross Trail, eastbound in prairie bordered with wooded islands, to meet the spur trail left to Bee Island Campsite at 5.8 miles. At 5.9 miles, reach the pine- and oak-wooded camp with lantern post, tent sites, fire rings, and a pump well. This is a good first night's destination. Next day, backtrack and rejoin the Bee Island Cross Trail east to immediately intersect and turn right onto Bee Island Road. Long prairie vistas stretch to the south.

Cross Powerline Road at 7.0 miles and then cut through a wooded hammock, joining Pine Level Road. At 8.5 miles, meet the Myakka Trail in a tree stand. Head left, easterly on single-track, winding in and out of a line of trees. At 9.5 miles, a spur trail goes 0.1 mile to attractive Honore Campsite, set in a palm/oak hammock. From here, wander easterly, avoiding wetland depressions pocking the prairie. At 11.0 miles, cross South Powerline Road and keep easterly, enjoying the long vistas. At 12.2 miles, cross an unnamed fire road and then meet the Bobcat Cross Trail in woods at 12.4 miles. Stay right with the Myakka Trail, southbound, running alongside wet depressions, weaving in and out of woods, crossing a canal at 12.9 miles.

The Myakka Trail turns east to meet the spur trail to Panther Point Campsite at 13.9 miles, set in an oak, pine, and palm hammock. Leave the hammock and circle around a wetland. Cut through a pine grove to cross Deer Prairie Lane at 15.2 miles. Wander through a mix of prairie, ponds, and woods, crossing Deer Prairie Cut along the way. At 16.2 miles, come to the outflow of Deer Prairie Slough. There may or may not be a bridge here. The water should be flowing as you cross. The Myakka Trail works northeasterly along Deer Prairie Slough, a bona fide wooded wetland with cypress and willow trees. You will be amid hardwood hammocks as well as on the edge of woods with the slough to your left and prairie to your right. Stay with the blazes.

At 17.6 miles, the Myakka Trail, alternately referred to at this juncture as the East Loop, goes right, but we stay left with the Slough Cross Trail. Continue bordering Deer Prairie Slough, with land sloping up to prairie on your right, emerging at Old Railroad Grade at 18.2 miles. Keep north past the raised roadbed and meet the other end of the Myakka Trail/East Loop at 19.0 miles. You are on the edge of woods and prairie. Rejoin the Myakka Trail and, at 19.3 miles, bridge a canal in woods and then, at 19.4 miles, reach another signed intersection. Here, head right toward Oak Grove Campsite, traveling north and then joining a sand road east. At 19.7 miles, turn right into a shady live oak hammock and the fine Oak Grove Campsite, which has a pump well. This is a recommended second day's camp.

Next day, return to the Myakka Trail and head southwest along the north side of Deer Prairie Slough, enjoying the melding of forest and grasses, sometimes in the shade and sometime in the open. At 20.9 miles, cross North Deer Prairie Lane and turn west, beginning a long stretch of pure prairie hiking, snaking between occasional ponds, nearing some potential wet trailbed. At 23.0 miles, meet the north end of the Bobcat Cross Trail. Keep west on the Myakka Trail, still in prairie. Cut through a tree belt at 0.2 mile before crossing an unnamed fire road at 23.9 miles.

At 24.9 miles, meet the other end of the Bee Island Cross Trail. Keep north, playing tag with fire roads on open prairie presenting far-reaching views. Enter woods before meeting the spur trail left to popular and closest-to-the-trailhead Mossy Hammock Campsite set in a palm/oak hammock, at 27.6 miles. The site is pretty, but bring your own water. Just ahead, cross Mossy Island Road and keep north in attractive forest, coming along Mossy Island Slough.

At 28.6 miles, stay left with the Myakka Trail as an alternate route heads north to run along Clay Gully and pop out on the main park road after a mile. The Myakka Trail turns southwest in woods. At 29.0 miles, return to Fox's High Road. From here, turn right and backtrack 0.2 mile, completing the backpacking adventure at 29.2 miles.

## Mileages

- 0.0   Fox's High Road trailhead
- 1.1   Myakka Trail crosses Fox's Lower Road
- 5.0   Left on Bee Island Cross Trail
- 5.9   Bee Island Campsite

8.5     Rejoin Myakka Trail
9.5     Spur left to Honore Campsite
12.4    Meet the Bobcat Cross Trail in woods
13.9    Spur right to Panther Point Campsite
16.2    Cross the outflow of Deer Prairie Slough
17.6    Stay left with Slough Cross Trail
19.7    Oak Grove Campsite
23.0    Pass north end of Bobcat Cross Trail
24.9    Pass east end of Bee Island Cross Trail
27.6    Spur to Mossy Hammock Campsite
28.6    Spur leads right to Clay Gully
29.2    Fox's High Road trailhead

## Practice Trail Etiquette

We associate backpacking with wild places. But even when you are in the back of beyond, a certain decorum is expected of backpackers. After all, we don't want to be inconsiderate just because we are beyond the glare of an electric light. Keep the following considerations in mind concerning proper trail behavior.

Whether you're on a county, state, or national park trail, always remember that great care and resources (from God's handiwork as well as from your tax dollars) have gone into creating these trails. Don't deface trail signs or trees. It takes a long time for trees to grow big enough to be carved into. There's no need to let passersby know that you were here.

Hike on open trails only. Respect trail and road closures. Ask if you are not sure. There's usually a valid reason if a trail is closed—storm damage, mudslides, wildlife breeding area, etc. Avoid possible trespassing on private land. Imagine if that private land were yours. Obtain all permits and authorizations as required. For example, this trip at Myakka River State Park requires a backcountry permit for overnight backpacking.

Leave only footprints. Be sensitive to the ground beneath you. This also means staying on the existing trail and not blazing any new trails. Mudholes get wider and wider if walked around by everyone.

Have you ever reached a scenic spot only to find trash accompanying your view? Pack out what you pack in—and more. No one likes to see the trash someone else has left behind.

Never spook wildlife. An unannounced approach, a sudden movement, or a loud noise startles most animals. A surprised animal can be dangerous to you, to others, and to themselves. Give them plenty of space. After all, the wilderness is the only home they have.

Honor leash laws. Most trails require keeping your dog on a 6-foot leash. Some pet owners think their dog is special, outside any regulations, thus leash laws don't apply. I can't tell you how many times I've been jumped on by a dog with muddy feet while their owners are simultaneously yelling at their barking canine, creating a chaotic and unpleasant scene for everyone. Think of your fellow backpackers before setting your dog free. Unleashed dogs will also chase wildlife and perhaps become lost.

Plan ahead. Know your equipment, your ability, and the area where you are hiking—then prepare accordingly. Be self-sufficient at all times; carry necessary supplies for changes in weather or other conditions. Most backpacking accidents/rescues start with ill-prepared hikers overestimating their abilities. They become tired or worried, then make poor decisions, turning a bad situation worse. In contrast, a well-executed backpacking adventure is a satisfaction to you and to others. It builds your confidence and makes you want to backpack again.

Finally, be courteous to other hikers, bikers, and equestrians you encounter on the trails. Here at Myakka River State Park, hikers, bicyclists, and equestrians share some of the trails. Bikers should yield to hikers and equestrians. Hikers should yield to equestrians. If encountering a horse, get well off the trail, be still, and talk in smooth tones. Horses can sometimes be scared of hikers with packs on, so if wearing a pack, step to the lower side of the trail to make yourself seem smaller.

A little etiquette at home—and on the trail—can go a long way to smooth out the rough patches in life.

# 34

## Myakka State Forest Backpack

### Overview

Make a satisfying circuit on double-track trails, visiting quality reservable backcountry campsites at this attractive state forest situated along the lower Myakka River. From the trailhead, you'll tramp south to the Pine Straw Campsite, set in evergreens by a canal. Next day, circle around the preserve to the north and the Myakka River, where two riverside campsites make for excellent overnighting experiences. Close the loop the last day with more trekking among evergreens.

---

**Distance & Configuration**: 14.0-mile loop with spurs
**Difficulty**: Moderate, does have one short bushwhack
**Outstanding Features**: Great campsites, easy, well-marked trails
**Scenery**: 4
**Solitude**: 3
**Family-Friendly**: 3
**Canine-Friendly**: 3
**Fees/Permits**: Fee campsites
**Best Season**: November through March
**Maps**: Myakka State Forest
**For More Info**: Myakka State Forest, 2555 South River Rd, Englewood, FL 34223, 941-460-1333, https://www.fdacs.gov/; Campsite reservations: https://www.reserveamerica.com/
**Finding the Trailhead**: From exit 191, North Port, Englewood, on I-75, take River Road, CR 777, south for 9.4 miles to turn left into Myakka State Forest. Drive for 1.2 miles on Shell Road to the grassy trailhead parking on your left just after passing state forest headquarters. GPS trailhead coordinates: 26.987183, -82.285980

---

This backpack takes place on a handsome, preserved tract nearly encircled by civilization. We should appreciate these 8,593 acres set on a peninsula

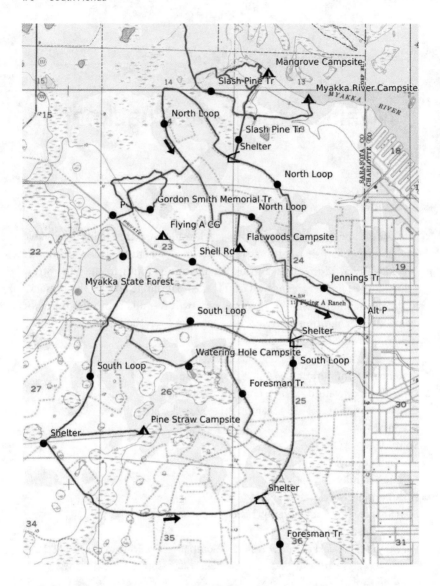

with a segment directly on the Myakka River, with two campsites beside the waterway, among the total of five backcountry campsites available for reservation. Former ranch- and farmland, the State of Florida purchased the parcel back in 1995; thus protected from development, it has become an alluring state forest where we can execute the fine art of backpacking.

You must reserve your campsites before your trip. The Myakka River Campsite is by far the most popular camp. Weekends are reserved well in advance. The other sites are generally available, but reservations in advance

Taking a break en route to the Myakka River.

can deliver peace of mind. If you reserve a site, your party has the camp to themselves. At most campsites, water can be had from nearby sources, but you may want to get your water from the Myakka River on an outgoing tide. It's always best to bring in your own water if you want to be positive about availability and purity of the source.

The trails are all double-track, making them easy to follow and trek upon, allowing you to focus on your surroundings instead of every footfall. The South Loop is a little wetter and has spots where you may get your feet wet while winding your way among prairie ponds. The recommended backpack can be a fun and easy two-nighter or a moderate one-night adventure. Leave the parking area and walk east down Shell Road for just a short distance and then head right, southbound on the South Loop. Almost all the trails are open to hikers, bicyclers, and equestrians, so be aware. Work around a gate and then tramp along an elevated trail bordered by pines. Numbered posts correspond to the downloadable map to help keep you apprised of your position. Be watchful of additional unblazed fire roads and other tracks.

At 0.7 mile, reach the loop portion of the South Loop. If you head left, it is 0.2 mile to the Foresman Trail and then another 0.6 mile to the Watering Hole Campsite, set in a grassy area bordered by woods next to a small pond with a little ramp. Like all the campsites, this one has a fire ring and picnic table. Our hike keeps straight, southbound, on the South Loop. Scrub oaks and palmetto join the pines. At 1.8 miles, take the signed left for the Pine Straw Campsite, heading east in a menagerie of palm, wax myrtle, prairie, and pine. At 2.5 miles, reach the camp, set against a perennial canal in pines and grasses with vegetated spoil from the water-filled canal creating a few small hills in the area. Water is easily had from the canal.

Next day, backtrack to the South Loop and head south, spanning the canal on a hiker bridge at 3.2 miles. Open onto a clearing with a trail kiosk. Stay with the South Loop, now heading east into increasingly open lands with prairie and wetland depressions, and small ponds. The trail by these ponds may be sloppy. Tree cover is sporadic. At 5.2 miles, reach an intersection in now thicker woods. Note the sun/storm shelter here, complete with a forest map. At this junction, the Foresman Trail leaves right to the Foresman Boulevard trailhead. We continue the South Loop Trail, entering a wet, grassy depression, almost sure to wet your shoes. You are across the marsh at 5.4 miles, and at 5.6 miles, in now richer forest, the Foresman Trail heads northwest for the Watering Hole Campsite. We keep north on a now elevated track bordered by small ditches, making for dry, often grassy hiking.

At 6.4 miles, the South Loop turns left at a sun shelter. Pay close attention here. Head left, west, just a short distance and then split right, northbound on an unmarked double-track. The mown track dead-ends ahead, but you keep north, passing to the right of a grassy depression marsh on an overgrown track that is barely discernable. You may have to full-on bushwhack, but you can't mess up if you keep north—no matter what, you will run into Shell Road. Oddly enough, pass an old power pole and keep north to emerge on Shell Road at 6.8 miles.

Once at Shell Road, turn right, easterly on the packed gravel track, to reach the Jennings trailhead at 7.2 miles. Here, head left on the single-track needle-carpeted Jennings Trail, winding northwesterly under a bushy canopy of pines. At 7.9 miles, meet the North Loop. If you go left here, it is 0.7

mile to the spur left to Flatwoods Campsite and 0.3 mile farther at the dead end of a spur. There is no easy nearby water source to go along with the fire ring and picnic table at Flatwoods Campsite.

Our backpack heads north on the North Loop. At 9.0 miles, intersect the Slash Pine Trail. There is a sun/storm shelter here as well. Head right, north on the Slash Pine Trail, trekking through pine woods, passing a wetland on your left. At 9.3 miles, head right toward the coveted Myakka River Campsite, jogging north just before reaching the camp at 10.0 miles. Here, interspersed pines rise over a grassy clearing, presenting first-rate river views—especially at sunset. A dock protrudes into the river, where boat campers also access the campsite. This is a fine and heavily used camp.

From here, backtrack to the Slash Pine Trail; then turn north toward the Mangrove Campsite, reached at 11.0 miles, primarily bordered by palms, pines, and live oaks. The campsite is not directly alongside the water, but it is close. Mangrove Campsite is in less demand than is Myakka River Campsite. Now it is time to backtrack to the North Loop, reached at 11.7 miles. The last part of the circuit backpack is easy as you tread north then curve back south. At 13.3 miles, split right toward the trailhead on a wide sand track. Cross the Gordan Smith Memorial Nature Trail twice; then cut left as it seems you are going directly into the forest headquarters. Pop out just east of the parking area, completing the gratifying circuit backpack at 14.0 miles.

## Mileages

| | |
|---|---|
| 0.0 | Myakka State Forest trailhead |
| 0.7 | South Loop goes left toward Watering Hole Campsite |
| 1.8 | Left toward Pine Straw Campsite |
| 2.5 | Pine Straw Campsite |
| 5.2 | Foresman Trail leaves right |
| 6.8 | Right on Shell Road |
| 7.2 | Left on Jennings Trail |
| 9.0 | Right on Slash Pine Trail |
| 10.0 | Myakka River Campsite |
| 11.0 | Mangrove Campsite |
| 11.7 | Continue North Loop |
| 14.0 | Return to Myakka State Forest trailhead |

# 35

## Collier-Seminole Backpack

### Overview

This short but challenging backpack traverses pinelands, wooded swamps, and mangrove stands. The appropriately named Adventure Trail is subject to inundation on just about any part of the circuit. The first part is the driest part of the trek; then you take a spur to a backcountry campsite with live oaks, still recovering from hurricane damage. Next, work through the wetter, tougher part of the trek. The last part crosses challenging mangrove wetlands, with spongy soil. Expect navigational challenges despite frequent trail blazing.

---

**Distance & Configuration**: 7.5-mile loop with spur to campsite
**Difficulty**: Difficult due to wetlands, navigation, and dense vegetation
**Outstanding Features**: Swamp hiking, mangrove woods
**Scenery**: 4
**Solitude**: 4
**Family-Friendly**: 1
**Canine-Friendly**: 0
**Fees/Permits**: Fee campsite
**Best Season**: December through March
**Maps**: Collier-Seminole State Park
**For More Info**: Collier-Seminole State Park, 20200 Tamiami Trail East, Naples, FL 34114, 239-394-3397, https://www.floridastateparks.org/
**Finding the Trailhead**: From exit 101 on I-75 near Naples, take FL 84 south for 6.8 miles to turn left on US 41 south. Follow US 41 south for 8.4 miles to turn right into the main state park entrance. Enter the state park on your right. Head to the ranger station, pay your backcountry camping fee, and get the combination to the locked parking area. Return to US 41 and head south for 0.5 mile. Look left for the turn onto the signed trailhead road. Open the combination gate, continuing 0.2 mile to dead-end at the trailhead. GPS trailhead coordinates: 25.990011, -81.578413

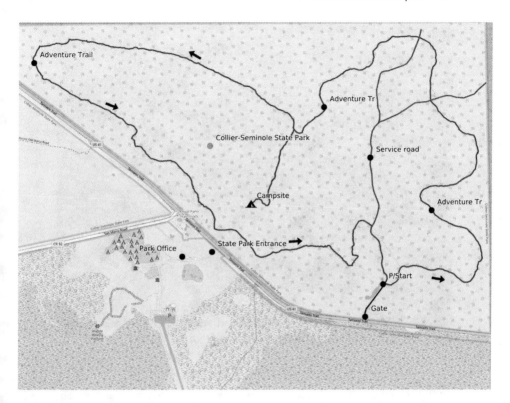

The Adventure Trail is aptly named. It is about guaranteed to be an adventure for backpackers. You will swamp-slog for sure and perhaps see some wildlife out here, from bear to deer to wild hogs. The path is well marked but can be difficult to follow in places, especially among fallen trees, wet areas, and thick, overgrown locales. This is strictly a winter-only backpack. Summer would be a hellish, high-water, bug-infested torture chamber. I recommend calling ahead and inquiring about water levels and overall trail conditions before attempting the hike. Speaking of water, remember to bring your own water to the campsite. Also, stay with the blazes, and if you lose them, backtrack until you spot the next blaze.

Join the single-track blazed Adventure Trail, leaving right from the trailhead, amid scrub oaks, palm, slash pine, mangrove, coco plum, and sawgrass. The forest will continually morph throughout the hike—one of the beauties of this overnighter.

By 0.3 mile, pass through a pine stand with sawgrass understory. At 0.5 mile, the path cuts through a dense cypress strand, returning to pines, typical of this ever-changing wildland. At 1.7 miles, the Adventure Trail crosses a service road and then keeps north, bisecting a small prairie to find a cypress

This is the most challenging short backpack in this guide.

strand. The trail becomes lower and wetter. Note the plant known as alligator flag, always an indicator of wetlands. Resume pines before reaching a second, elevated service road at 2.0 miles (if you head left on this service road, it is 1.2 miles back to the trailhead). The trail is turning westerly here, staying within Collier-Seminole State Park boundaries.

At 2.7 miles, cut through a tall cypress strand. Generally speaking, the taller the cypress trees, the deeper the water in the cypress stand. At 2.8 miles, take the spur leading left to the backcountry campsite. Work south, crossing a cypress/maple strand; then, at 3.2 miles, reach the simple camp in a recovering palm/live oak hammock. Shade is returning to this area that fell victim first to hurricanes, then to fire. But the state park does keep the site mown as shade trees continue to rise.

The second day's hike is harder. Return to the main loop at 3.6 miles. Head left among young slash pines, mixed in with taller evergreens. At 4.1 miles, enter a long trail section that is more cypress than not. Swamp-slogging is the norm. Depending upon water levels, you will be either sloshing in water or slopping in mud. It is part of backpacking "within one of the largest mangrove swamps in the world," as the Collier-Seminole State Park website states (even though this particular park section is more freshwater swamp than mangrove swamp). Unfortunately, some of these cypress areas will also host Brazilian pepper, creating scenically appealing dark woodlands, but the pepper crowds out the native vegetation, though plenty of bromeliads and ferns do remain. You may find yourself bending over while hiking through these low-roofed pepper thickets.

The going will be easier in the more open stretches. At 4.9 miles, the trail begins curving south, then east into cypress heavy woods, mixed with scattered live oaks and laurel oaks. It's crazy—you are walking through forest primeval yet you can hear cars on US 41 to your right. In some places brush rises among fallen trees, creating very challenging conditions.

At 5.7 miles, the Adventure Trail gets very adventurous as you cross frequent cypress strands. At 6.4 miles, the path begins crossing several mangrove-lined sloughs, some of them bridged with short boardwalks. Be very careful with your footing as you can sink deep into the mangrove sloughs. The trail is very mushy between the boardwalks. At 6.6 miles, a bridge mercifully takes you across the biggest slough. At 6.9 miles, the path unexpectedly turns north in a confusing area—look for blazes. You may have to fight through some sawgrass. Shortly open onto pine, and the walking greatly eases. At 7.2 miles, reach a service road. Turn right here, following the unbelievably easy double-track back to the trailhead, completing the adventure at 7.4 miles.

## Mileages

0.0   Trailhead
1.7   Cross service road
2.0   Cross second service road
2.8   Left on campsite spur
3.2   Backcountry campsite
4.9   Curve back toward trailhead
6.4   Cross mangrove sloughs
7.4   Trailhead

### Strategies for Dealing with Insects

Biting insects can be a challenge for Florida backpackers, especially during warmer, wetter weather. No matter how bad it gets, think about the advantages we have now—chemical repellents, tightly knit clothing, and fine tent netting—over the Calusa Indians who once roamed Southwest Florida.

Back then, the Calusa, scantily clad to tolerate the nearly year-round Everglades heat, coated their bodies with a pungent mixture of fish oil and pine tar. Those two ingredients didn't repel the "swamp angels," as mosquitoes are affectionately known in the Glades, but simply formed a thick layer on the skin through which bugs couldn't bite. That means the Calusa were still harassed by hordes of buzzing insects wherever they went.

Imagine being buzzed in your ears day after day, hour after hour, minute after minute. Today's Florida backpackers go about combating insects differently. For starters, we don't have to coat ourselves with stinky elixirs. Instead, I suggest using clothes as your first line of defense against biting naggers.

Starting at your feet, wear full shoes, thick socks, then long pants, even if the temperatures are warm. Don't go too thin in your clothes, either; skeeters will simply bite through them.

A long-sleeve shirt and a bandanna around your neck provide a protective barrier between your skin (under which is the coveted blood supply) and the bugs.

This leaves your head and hands exposed and is where bug dope comes in. I recommend real repellent, the chemical kind, with DEET. Citrus-based and other "natural" repellents smell good but do not work when the bugs are really bad. On a typical backpack I carry a lesser repellent, with 5–10 percent DEET or Picaridin, for lesser bug problems, as well as a smaller bottle of 50 percent or more DEET for when things get crazy.

Even at that, you may have to spray repellent directly on your socks or soak a bandanna in dope and then tie it around your neck for additional protection. Be careful applying repellent around your face and eyes. It will burn.

And if you use your hands in applying dope, realize it is going to get on everything you touch for a while, including food, cigars, drink cups, etc. I can tell you firsthand that DEET doesn't taste too good. So plan your application when possible around eating, drinking, and smoking.

Moreover, if things get really bad, consider a head net, which looks like it sounds. Head nets are mosquito netting that drapes over your head and can be cinched at the neck. These can be hot and will make claustrophobics quite uneasy, but they work.

In addition to clothing and bug dope, do as the Calusa did—use breezes to your advantage. Find campsites facing the wind. Then place your tent door into the breeze, keeping skeeters from aggregating at the door and getting in the tent during your entry and exit. Avoid being outside your tent during the "bug hours," dusk and dawn. Wear light clothing—bugs are less attracted to bright colors.

If you use the above, backpacking in Florida can be a lot more pleasant—and you will smell better than the Calusa.

# 36

## Big Cypress Backpack

### Overview

This backpack of extremes is Florida's most watery, most difficult, and certainly most unusual 30 miles of trail trekking. Situated in Big Cypress National Preserve, this adventure leads you through an ultra-remote segment of South Florida through cypress swamps, pinelands, and hardwood hammocks, though most of the adventure entails "swamp-slogging" through cypress and sawgrass. Several designated and other undesignated campsites enhance the possibilities.

**Distance & Configuration**: 31.5-mile end-to-end
**Difficulty**: Difficult due to distance and miles of walking through water
**Outstanding Features**: Stunning scenery, challenge, remoteness
**Scenery**: 5
**Solitude**: 4
**Family-Friendly**: 0
**Canine-Friendly**: 0
**Fees/Permits**: Free backpacking permit required, available online
**Best Season**: Mid-December through March
**Maps**: Big Cypress National Preserve
**For More Info**: Big Cypress National Preserve, Oasis Visitor Center, 52105 Tamiami Trail East, Ochopee, FL 34141, 239-695-4111, https://www.nps.gov/bicy/index.htm
**Finding the Trailhead**: The northern trailhead for this backpack is located at mile marker 63 rest area on I-75 between Naples and Fort Lauderdale. Specific NPS parking is located on the western end of the rest area facility on the north side of the interstate. To reach the hike's beginning, return to I-75 north and drive 16 miles to exit 80 and take FL 29 south for 17.3 miles. Then turn left onto US 41 south and follow it for 21.2 miles to turn left into Oasis Visitor Center. GPS trailhead coordinates: I-75, mile marker 63: 26.169355, -81.077998; Oasis Visitor Center: 25.857337, -81.032759

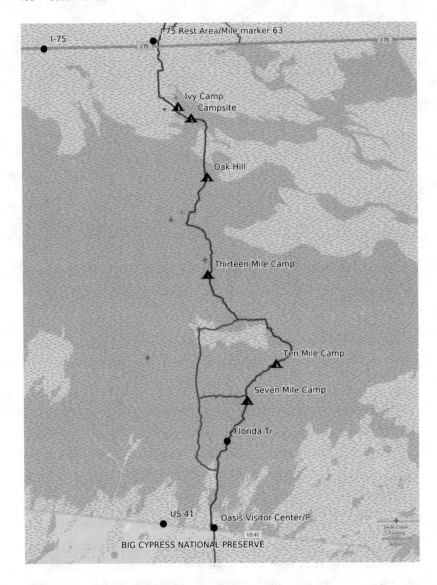

This is Florida's backpack of superlatives—the most challenging, the most wet, and the most unique backpacking trip not only in Florida but in the lower 48. Here, follow the Florida Trail as it winds amid wet cypress sloughs, sawgrass prairies, and pine islands covered in palmetto in the heart of the endangered Florida panther's habitat, 700,000-acre Big Cypress National Preserve. You will comprehend the meaning of "big" in the Big Cypress after trekking miles and miles of cypress sloughs, punctuated by slash pine/sabal palm hammocks and rich tropical hardwood hammocks.

There is no other backpacking experience like that in the Big Cypress.

The backpacking is very challenging. You are guaranteed wet feet and slogging through water up to your knees. Some sections present miles of unbroken trekking through water in bald cypress stands with no place to stop. Irregular limestone rock, cypress knees, and silty mud will challenge your footfalls. Be mentally and physically prepared when entering the Big Cypress. You will cross swamp buggy trails, but other than that it is you and the elements out here.

Five designated first-come, first-served backcountry campsites add to the trip possibilities. However, you may camp anywhere in the Big Cypress as long as it is ½ mile from a developed area or road. In practice, this will include only the dry lands through which you backpack. I recommend this as a three-night backpack. Travel is slow. Enjoy the setting, take your time, and hike with care.

The starting point for this backpack is also the southern terminus of the entire Florida Trail, Oasis Visitor Center. Leave from the rock with the Florida Trail plaque near the front entrance and head west along the US 41 canal. Soon turn right, still following the fence line bordering a small airstrip, northbound on an elevated berm cut by shallow channels, where you will wet your feet the first time. Your shoes will remain wet the entire trek—bring camp shoes. Palms, wax myrtle, and small cypress border the trail with sawgrass extending in the distance.

The water through which you walk is quite clear—until you step in it. Reach the first pine island at 1.0 miles, where tall slash pines shade palms and palmettos. At 1.4 miles, a spur trail goes right to a swamp buggy trail. The trail alternates between drier pine/palm hammocks and wet cypress/sawgrass complexes, in a seeming tug-of-war between dry and wet tree species. This ceaseless morphing of ecosystems will continue throughout the trek.

You will learn to watch the hole-pocked limestone at your feet while admiring the changing landscape. At 3.0 miles, pass a gate and private property sign, though the landscape remains unchanged, dominated by pines in one area then cypress in another. In drier areas you may find small trailside camps where backpackers have thrown down.

Cross a pair of cypress strands at 4.1 miles. These cypress strands generally have deeper water and taller trees. At 4.3 miles, pass a hardwood hammock to your left. You can see live oaks rising overhead. Bird life is abundant throughout the Big Cypress. Expect to go through burned areas, even the cypress stands. At 6.9 miles, come to a big pine island and, at 7.0 miles, to signed Seven Mile Camp. It is set in a pine/myrtle/palmetto woods and features a fire ring, picnic table, and scattered tent sites. Water can be had from a nearby cypress dome.

Trek through pines with occasional wetter areas with coco plum and cypress, crossing a buggy trail at 7.6 miles. The vegetation in this flat land changes with the slightest changes in elevation. At 8.0 miles, navigate a dry area with potholes galore. Ahead, cross more cypress strands in this most southerly backpack in this guide. At 9.3 miles, pass another signed private property inholding while cutting through a cypress strand. At 9.7 miles, come to an exceptionally large and wide pine island, finding signed Ten

Mile Camp just ahead. It offers a fire ring and picnic table with nearby tent sites. Water can be had from the cypress area just crossed.

Enjoy some dry pine walking before once again diving into cypress, where epiphytes cling to the trees. At 10.6 miles, the trail arcs northwest, entering a long area of cypress. At 12.4 miles, the trail circles around a sawgrass prairie to your left. Beyond there, continue tracing the blazes through mixed landscape of prairies, cypress woods, and pine islands. Palms become more prevalent on drier lands.

At 14.4 miles, curve northwesterly, here in the heart of the Big Cypress. Cruise some pinelands with small scattered prairies. Stay with the blazes as the trail plays tag with a buggy road. Ahead, the landscape changes continually—pine, cypress, and every mix of the two. At 17.2 miles, enter a hardwood hammock of live oak, palm, and pine, reaching signed Thirteen Mile Camp. Even from a distance, this tree island is thicker than those previously passed. This fine, shady campsite includes a picnic table and metal fire ring, with scattered tent sites. Surrounding cypress domes hold water.

The Florida Trail streams north from Thirteen Mile Camp to cross a swamp buggy road and enter a cypress slough. Continue the pattern of trekking through sloughs and crossing palm/pine hammocks. Though the trail makes many twists and turns, it keeps a generally northward course through a montage of cypress and pine. Numerous tall cypress domes rise on the horizon. Cross occasional swamp buggy roads. At 20.4 miles, the Florida Trail curves alongside an old barbed wire fence to the left. Come near hardwood hammocks but stay in dwarf bald cypress rising from sawgrass. At 23.3 miles, come to signed Oak Hill Camp. Live oaks, manchineel, Simpson stopper, ferns, and coco plum grow thickly around the shady, closed-in camping area. It offers tent sites and fire ring.

From here on out, the trail is unbroken cypress trekking save for a couple of island hammocks. Get your mojo on. Continue north through a sea of cypress dotted with small tree islands and cypress domes creating an undulating landscape. This is where you'll find out what the Big Cypress is all about, a pale ghost world of white trees rising from tan sawgrass. Keep slogging through cypress of differing sizes and shapes, with bigger cypresses having deeper water.

You will be teased, coming near hammock islands but not on them. At 26.8 miles, skirt by a small hammock island with a small campsite carved out from it, the first accessible dry land in miles. Continue in cypress to reach signed Ivy Camp at 27.4 miles. This cleared isle is surrounded by cypress swamp. The shaded small camp has tent sites and openings onto the cypress, more open than not, nary a stick of firewood. Resume swampslogging, with almost all cypress on the horizon. Bisect a few buggy tracks.

At 28.9 miles, cross sawgrass prairies with palm islands in the distance. At 29.4 miles swing around a pine hammock and then join a dry hardwood hammock of live oak, palm, and pine at 29.6 miles. By this point you may have forgotten how to walk on dry land. Cruelly, make an abrupt right turn to the east off the terra firma and then come to the main buggy road connecting to I-75. Turn left and follow the wide, muddy trail north, staying with the orange blazes before coming to a high metal fence with a gate at 31.0 miles. You are in the southeast quadrant of the large rest stop area. From here, head left, go under the interstate, and turn right to reach the rest stop hiker parking area, adding 0.5 mile to the backpack.

## Mileages

  0.0   Oasis Visitor Center
  7.0   Seven Mile Camp
  9.8   Ten Mile Camp
 17.2   Thirteen Mile Camp
 23.3   Oak Hill Camp
 26.8   Small campsite
 27.4   Ivy Camp
 29.4   Dry hammock
 31.0   Gate
 31.5   I-75 Rest stop building parking area

# 37

# Big Cypress North Loop Backpack

## Overview

Make a circuit through the northern Big Cypress using the Florida Trail and other paths to explore untamed South Florida. Several campsites along the route expand opportunities. Furthermore, cross trails allow you to adjust the loop. Start by following old Nobles Grade—now the Florida Trail—past a changing landscape of pines, palms, and cypress. Find shady Nobles Camp and then loop through live oak hammocks, palmetto prairies, and wetland marshes to Panther Camp, set in high pines. Complete the circuit, passing open Carpenter Camp.

---

**Distance & Configuration**: 15.3-mile balloon loop
**Difficulty**: Moderate, does have a few wet sections
**Outstanding Features**: First-rate scenery, good campsites, mostly dry footing
**Scenery**: 5
**Solitude**: 3
**Family-Friendly**: 3
**Canine-Friendly**: 4
**Fees/Permits**: No fees or permits required
**Best Season**: Mid-December through early April
**Maps**: Big Cypress National Preserve
**For More Info**: Big Cypress National Preserve, Oasis Visitor Center, 52105 Tamiami Trail East, Ochopee, FL 34141, 239-695-4111, https://www.nps.gov/bicy/index.htm
**Finding the Trailhead**: The trailhead for this backpack is located at mile marker 63 rest area on I-75 between Naples and Fort Lauderdale. Specific NPS parking is located on the western end of the rest area facility on the north side of the interstate. However, the hike starts at the fence in the northeastern end of the rest stop area, north of the interstate and east of rest stop on that side (there is also a rest stop on the south side of I-75). GPS trailhead coordinates: 26.169364, -81.072737

---

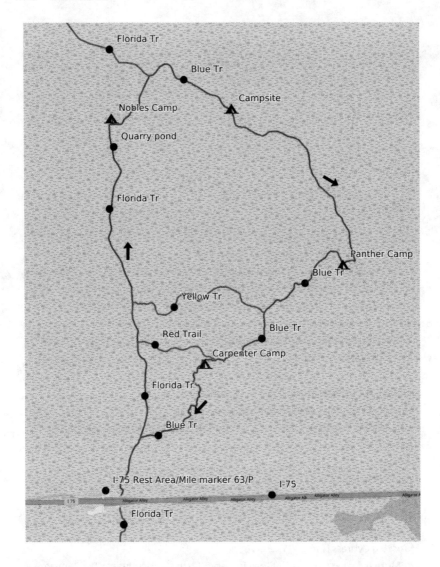

This circuit backpack presents a chance to explore wild, beautiful, and fabled Big Cypress National Preserve on drier trails than on the southern end of the uncultivated land. A well-marked and -maintained trail network, along with good campsites, make executing an overnight adventure here much easier than trekking through the heart of the Big Cypress, with its challenging swamp-slogging and long-distance commitment.

Your feet stand a much better chance of staying dry here in the northern Big Cypress. The first part of the loop follows the Florida Trail, overlain on Nobles Grade, an old road leading to a remote airstrip. The footing is dry as

Author relaxing at Panther Camp.

you parallel a canal, passing cross trails shortcutting the greater loop. After nearly 5 miles, come to Noble Camp, set under oaks. Ahead, the loop leaves the Florida Trail, tracing also-dry Jones Grade to reach fine Panther Camp, set in a grassy flat bordered in pines. The last part of the loop is where you'll end up with wet feet, as it passes palmetto prairies and grassy wetlands, as well as cypress swamps. Carpenter Camp is dry, however, in scant pines and some palms. The route can be either a one-nighter or an easy two-nighter, perfect for families or backpackers who just want to take it easy. The cross trails can shorten the trek even more.

Start the circuit by passing through a wire gate with the Florida Trail logo on it. Join Nobles Grade and reach a kiosk and sign-in log. Keep straight, north on double-track Nobles Grade over which runs the Florida Trail. The elevated dry track, an old oil-exploration road, runs alongside coco plum, wax myrtle, and palms, with green pinelands and pale cypress domes in the distance.

At 0.8 mile, your return route, the Blue Trail, enters on the right. Stay straight on the wide and easy Florida Trail. Game trails cross the track. At 2.0 miles, the 1.4-mile Red Trail splits right. Keep north on the Florida Trail, reaching the Yellow Trail at 2.5 miles. It leaves right at 2.1 miles to bisect the greater loop.

The Florida Trail continues meandering north amid pines and palms, then opens into some sawgrass. At 4.5 miles, pass a quarry pond to your right; then curve right at 4.8 miles to quickly reach an intersection. Here, a 0.1-mile spur leads left to a field and signed path left into oak-shaded Nobles Camp with picnic table and fire ring, bordered by palms, with good tent sites. Water can be had from a nearby small quarry pond. Continue the loop by backtracking from Nobles Camp and resuming the Florida Trail, cutting through a live oak hammock, rich with ferns, and with tree arms roofing the path. Unfortunately, you will also be seeing too much exotic Brazilian pepper.

At 5.8 miles, split right with the Blue Trail, as the Florida Trail aims for points north. You are now on another elevated berm, Jones Grade. Other old elevated logging tracks spur from the Blue Trail, but the correct way is blazed each time. Work southeast on the grassy double-track, piercing a menagerie of habitats typical of the Big Cypress. Don't be surprised if you see bear scat on the trail—this is among the best bruin habitat in South Florida. They love live oak acorns. At 7.0 miles, reach an unnamed campsite with a bench and fire ring. Per the rules at Big Cypress, you can disperse camp here. Ahead, a few old grades spur from the Blue Trail.

Pass a large sawgrass prairie just before the Blue Trail makes a hard right at a sign at 9.8 miles. Hike west, still circling the sawgrass prairie to reach signed Panther Camp at 10.0 miles. The main campsite has a fire ring and picnic table, with a less-used campsite behind it. Pines provide shade, and you can pitch your tent in nooks between palms. Get your water from the aforementioned sawgrass prairie.

The Blue Trail continues southwest in palmetto, gallberry, and wild rosemary prairies bordered by sawgrass wetlands. The grade deteriorates in places, especially near sawgrass, and is where you'll wet your feet. At 11.5 miles, meet the other end of the Yellow Trail. Stay with the Blue Trail, passing the other end of the Red Trail at 12.4 miles. Again, stay with the Blue Trail, weaving through palmettos, pines, and sawgrass to reach popular Carpenter Camp at 12.8 miles. It offers a picnic table, fire ring, and water from an adjacent cypress dome. A few pines and palms provide shade for the grassy campsite.

Continuing on, you'll pass near and through cypress strands, with a foot wetting likely. Cut through a live oak hammock and then merge into pines and palms on a single-track path. Stay with the blazes as it rejoins an old grade. Complete the loop at 14.5 miles and then backtrack 0.8 mile, finishing the backpack at 15.3 miles.

## Mileages

- 0.0   Mile marker 63 northeast trailhead
- 0.8   Stay left with Florida Trail
- 4.8   Spur left 0.1 mile to Nobles Camp
- 7.0   Unnamed campsite
- 10.0   Panther Camp
- 12.8   Carpenter Camp
- 15.3   Mile marker 63 northeast trailhead

### Night Hiking Is a Viable Option

Gusts of wind were pealing through the pines, whooshing sounds emanating from the swaying evergreens overhead, pine needles dropping all about. A front was blowing through the northern Big Cypress National Preserve, and I was miles from the Alligator Alley I-75 trailhead. Concerned about a change in already sullen January skies, I turned on my weather radio. It predicted showers moving in around daybreak. The radar on my phone confirmed a threatening line of storms heading my way. I was hiking out the next day and amended my plan in order to beat the rain back to my vehicle.

The new plan: night hiking. Yep, walking in the dark, strolling under the stars, trudging in the blackness. I broke camp at 5:00 a.m., strapped on my pack, and logged more than 3 miles before dawn lightened the skies, making the trailhead just as heavy rain reached my neck of the Big Cypress.

As fall progresses and winter approaches, we have fewer hours of daylight. Hikers should consider adapting to increased darkness. Using the hours after sunset or before sunrise for backpacking in Florida can make more trips happen. And isn't that what it's all about—making trips happen? In the above example I used night hiking simply to escape inclement weather. Consider adding night hiking to your backpacking arsenal.

Most night hiking is done after sunset, rather than before sunrise, especially on Friday evenings, when just-off-work backpackers race to the wilderness, hike to a given point, and set up camp under cover of darkness.

Even if you have the car packed, the pack loaded, and the grub bought, it's just hard to get out of work and to your destination before the sun drops in winter. There's the invariable last-minute stop, the wrong turn, and your sidekick being late again.

So what are the advantages of night hiking? First, you can simply travel when you want twenty-four hours a day, even if getting a late start, avoiding a rainstorm, or covering more miles than daylight allows. Night hiking presents a completely different experience—an often eerie one. Your auditory senses rise. Every sound of the woodlands seems amplified and takes on more meaning. Was that crack of a breaking stick or a bear coming? Was that rushing sound moving water or an unseen stranger talking? Is that loud splash an alligator or someone coming to get you?

Since your range of light is limited, you more closely notice what is near—footprints in a muddy section of trail, tree limbs reaching for your pack, or that pair of eyes reflecting just beyond.

Night hiking has plenty of disadvantages. First, you simply can't see as much of what you came to see. Also, you may miss landmarks, campsites, or trail junctions. Furthermore, there is simply an increased risk of taking a spill.

Travel by night has a way of seeming slow. Maybe because you can't tell where you are most of the time. When embarking on your first night hike, go somewhere with which you are already familiar. Get the feel of what it is like without bad consequences. Avoid rain and fog if possible. And make absolutely sure you have fresh/recharged batteries in your headlamp. In the final benefit vs. risk analysis, I will continue to use night hiking to enjoy more trails that lace the Sunshine State.

# 38

## Dupuis Loop Backpack

### Overview

Delivering a sense of remoteness and superlative beauty, this circuit backpack combines the Ocean-to-Lake Trail with connecting paths to make a loop through a menagerie of natural environments, delivering a sense of remoteness in the back of beyond. Two designated backcountry campsites allow you to vary your trip as a one- or two-night affair.

---

**Distance & Configuration**: 15.4-mile loop

**Difficulty**: Moderate, does have muddy sections

**Outstanding Features**: Remoteness, scenery

**Scenery**: 5

**Solitude**: 4

**Family-Friendly**: 1

**Canine-Friendly**: 1

**Fees/Permits**: None required

**Best season**: December through early April

**Maps**: Dupuis Wildlife Management Area

**For More Info**: Dupuis Wildlife Management Area, 23500 SW Kanner Highway, Canal Point, FL 33438, 561-924-5310, https://www.sfwmd.gov/

**Finding the Trailhead**: From exit 101 on I-95 west of Jupiter Island, take FL 76 west for 19.9 miles to Gate 1 of Dupuis WMA, then follow the sand road for 1 mile, passing the left turn into Dupuis Family Campground. Drive 0.6 mile beyond the Dupuis Family Campground entrance to turn left on a gravel road; shortly, dead-end at the Governors House Picnic Area, with a large parking area and a picnic shelter. GPS trailhead coordinates: 27.000535, -80.552785

---

Dupuis covers 21,835 wild acres east of Lake Okeechobee. Its pine woods, wetlands, and other habitats deliver a real sense of seclusion. You can enjoy this backwoods combining a segment of the long-distance Ocean-to-Lake Trail with a series of loops that link to the Ocean-to-Lake Trail. Two

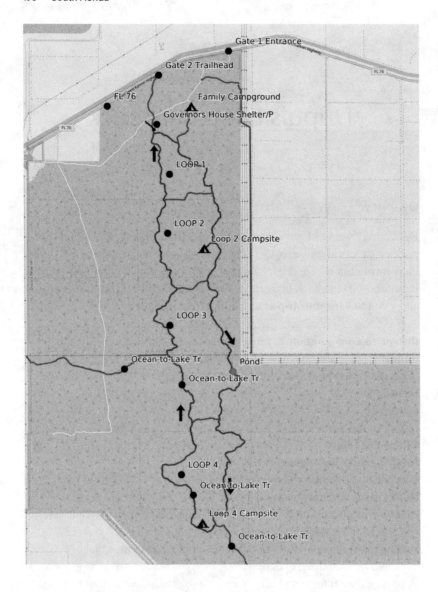

backcountry campsites along this circuit backpack allow you to fashion a one- or two-night trip. The Loop 2 Campsite is a first-come, first-served designated spot in pines and palms 2.3 miles into the adventure. Bring your own water. The Loop 4 Campsite, also first-come, first-served, offers picnic tables, fire rings, a pitcher pump, and benches under arrow-straight pines, with a small canal nearby.

The trails are well blazed and signed but can be brushy in places. You will pass through wet sections, but the pathway is more dry than not. Game

Lightweight netting used by the author in lieu of a tent.

trails and fire lanes intersect the track, and you sometimes follow fire lanes for a short period, but as long as you stay with the blazes you will be fine. Do not continue if you lose the blazes.

Leave south from the picnic area on a white-blazed path. All of the stacked loops in Dupuis except for the Ocean-to-Lake Trail are blazed in white. After a couple hundred feet, come to the first signed intersection. Head left on the east side of Loop 1. Enter mostly grass open terrain with scattered pine islands, wiregrass prairies, grassy depression marshes, fern pockets, palmetto thickets, and palm groves, along with cypress domes, a real patchwork quilt of ecosystems.

At 0.4 mile, a spur trail splits left to the Dupuis Family Campground. At 1.3 miles, cross a yellow-blazed equestrian trail (not shown on map). At 1.6 miles, reach an intersection. Here the cross trail for Loops 1 and 2 heads west. Stay left here, still on the east side of the loops. Just ahead, cross a second equestrian trail. The forest thickens a bit, providing more shade.

At 2.0 miles, a boardwalk leads over a shallow ditch. This is about the only help you are going to get crossing these shallow drainages, that were used to make lands better suited for cattle, timber, or crops. After working through a wet section, reach dry land. At 2.3 miles, a spur leads right 0.2 mile to the simple Loop 2 Campsite. It is set in a clearing bordered by palms and pines. Remember, bring your own water to this site.

The backpack continues south through a beautiful section of regal pines with scattered saw palmetto copses. The trail is much easier to follow. At 3.0 miles, skirt a grassy depression marsh to your right before reentering pines. At 3.2 miles, come to the cross trail for Loops 2 and 3. Stay straight, southbound; entering the back of beyond, in thicker stands of woods, skirting marshes and cypress domes. Mostly stay in belts of trees. At 4.7 miles, surprisingly come to a comma-shaped quarry pond, a scenic watery oasis nestled in the woods. Begin working around a series of cypress domes in wetter terrain.

At 5.7 miles, reach another junction. Here the cross trail of Loops 3 and 4 leaves right, but we stay straight, moving deeper into the hinterlands. Fern thickets are abundant. Enter low woods with cypress. At 7.6 miles, come alongside an old canal. The trail travels atop the sandy canal spoil. Then, at 7.9 miles, reach an intersection. Here, turn right, joining the Ocean-to-Lake Trail, lake-bound. Cross the canal by culvert and turn west. Wander through light young pines and then come to another elevated spoil and small canal to reach the Loop 4 Campsite at 8.1 miles. Here, a short spur leads to the recommended camp.

From Loop 4 Campsite, the Ocean-to-Lake Trail trucks north in the patchwork quilt vegetation that characterizes Dupuis. At 9.3 miles, pass through an area of cypress, along with pines and palms displaying wide bases to remain upright during wet periods. At 10.3 miles, the path leads through a shady live oak/pine/palm hammock. At 10.4 miles, stay left at the intersection with the cross trail of Loops 3 and 4.

At 11.6 miles, the Ocean-to-Lake Trail splits left along a huge grassy strip, bound for Lake Okeechobee. Our loop keeps straight, northbound, on a white-blazed trail that shows less use. Ahead, weave amid grassy depression marshes bordered by pinelands. Many of these marshes will have shallow outflow ditches through which you must walk.

At 12.9 miles, the cross trail of Loops 2 and 3 goes right, while we stay left, still on the west side of the Dupuis stacked loops, northbound. Myrtle and ferns grow alongside the trail. At 13.4 miles, cross an equestrian path. At 14.2 miles, the Loops 1 and 2 cross trail goes right. We stay straight. Oaks increase in number, yet the trail also crosses some wet, mushy areas. Reach the final intersection within sight of the Governors House Picnic Area. Here, backtrack the short distance, completing the backpack at 15.4 miles.

## Mileages

0.0   Governors House Picnic Area
1.6   Pass cross trail of Loops 1 & 2
2.3   Spur to Loop 2 Campsite
2.5   Loop 2 Campsite
3.2   Pass cross trail of Loops 2 & 3
5.7   Pass cross trail of Loops 3 & 4
7.9   Right on Ocean-to-Lake Trail
8.1   Loop 4 Campsite
10.4  Pass cross trail of Loops 3 & 4
11.6  Leave Ocean-to-Lake Trail
12.9  Pass cross trail of Loops 2 & 3
14.2  Pass cross trail of Loops 1 & 2
15.4  Governors House Picnic Area

# 39

## Bowman Island Backpack

### Overview

Follow a stretch of the Ocean-to-Lake Trail through big and wild Corbett Wildlife Management Area (WMA) to reach Bowman Island campsite, a semi-tropical hardwood hammock rising thick and lush amid a sea of pine stands and grassy marshes. The backpack involves some swamp-slogging and potential wildlife viewing.

---

**Distance & Configuration**: 12.2-mile there-and-back
**Difficulty**: Moderate-difficult due to swamp-slogging and mud-slopping
**Outstanding Features**: Hardwood hammock campsite, wetlands
**Scenery**: 4
**Solitude**: 4
**Family-Friendly**: 1
**Canine-Friendly**: 1
**Fees/Permits**: Daily use permit required
**Best Season**: December through March
**Maps**: J. W. Corbett Wildlife Management Area, Ocean-to-Lake Trail Map 3—Corbett
**For More Info**: J. W. Corbett Wildlife Management Area, South Region, 8535 Northlake Blvd, West Palm Beach, FL 33412, 561-625-5122, https://myfwc.com/
**Finding the Trailhead**: From Exit 77 on I-95 near North Palm Beach, take Northlake Boulevard west for 12.2 miles to turn right onto Seminole Pratt Whitney Road. Follow it for 2.9 miles to turn left onto Stumpers Grade Road, entering Corbett WMA. Follow it 0.6 mile; then, just before reaching the entrance gate of the Everglades Youth Camp, follow the signs left to Hungryland Boardwalk and Florida Trail hikers parking area and park there. GPS trailhead coordinates: 26.855947, -80.302339

---

Bowman Island is one of my favorite backcountry campsites in all of Florida. A dense-forested hammock of live oak, strangler fig, and pond apple along

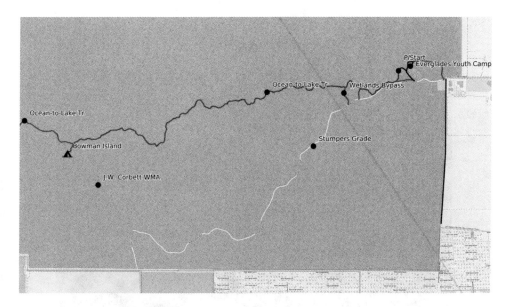

with ferns, wild coffee, and Simpsons stopper as well as orchids fashion a semi-tropical forested hideaway set in a greater expanse of pines and grassy wetlands. The campsite also has a fire ring and log "furniture."

And the hike to get there isn't too bad either—you trace the long-distance Ocean-to-Lake Trail the entire route. The well-blazed track leads through a pine flatwoods with palmetto and wax myrtle underneath the evergreens. The trail winds through these pines and astride wide, grassy marshes that open views to the horizon. The trail presents challenges, too. For along the grassy marshes you will encounter muddy pathway and sections that are underwater. Depending on whether it has been a wet year or not, the backpacking through Corbett WMA can be a pure swamp-slog or a light wetting, but count on wet feet when preparing—bring camp shoes and dry socks for Bowman Island. Also, during hunting season swamp, buggies barrel through the WMA, producing wide, muddy tracks that sometimes coincide with the Ocean-to-Lake Trail, creating navigational confusion. To counter this, the Florida Trail Association keeps the Ocean-to-Lake Trail well blazed. Therefore, stick with the blazes and you'll be fine. That said, I guarantee you will be briefly discombobulated a time or two during the trek.

Corbett, more than 60,000 acres in size, is one of the largest wildlife management areas in South Florida, keeping this part of western Palm Beach County home to birds of the air and four-footed critters from deer to hogs. Corbett also is a part of the overall Everglades renewal project, an effort to restore the historic sheet flow of water to replicate conditions as they once were.

Sunrise on the Ocean-to-Lake Trail.

The backpack parking area, shared with the popular Hungryland Boardwalk, offers a small picnic shelter and restroom. Join a blue-blazed trail heading south from an informative kiosk. Enter pine flatwoods mixed with ferns, myrtle, coco plum, and saw palmetto. As with many trails in South Florida, the trailbed is grassy. At 0.1 mile, reach the Ocean-to-Lake Trail. Head right, westerly, lake-bound in pines and palms. Note the scattered cypress in the forest, also an indicator of seasonally inundated lands.

By 0.4 mile, you are skirting the edge of a grassy marsh. These wet prairies are interspersed with the pinelands throughout the hike, where sawgrass, St. Johns wort, and rushes rise thick from the water. At 0.8 mile, intersect the Wetlands Bypass. Here a white-blazed trail splits left through higher terrain, joins Stumpers Grade Road, then cuts back into the forest. The bypass does avoid one pure swamp-slog, but if it is a wet year, the bypass will be sloppy too. No matter the conditions, you can take it on your return trip to log new mileage.

The Ocean-to-Lake Trail leads directly through a grassy marsh. Once you get your feet wet, it is no big deal. The slog extends for 0.1 mile before you rise to pine flatwoods. At 1.1 miles, the other end of the Wetlands Bypass enters on your left. At 1.4 miles, pass under a wide power line. Continue west, weaving between grassy marshes while in pines and palms.

By this point you will have surmised whether it is a wet year or not. At 1.9 miles, the Ocean-to-Lake Trail has to thread the needle between two grassy marshes on either side of the path. Settle down into a pattern of woods walking and skirting marshes and occasionally navigating amid swamp buggy trails.

Keep eyes peeled for the exposed limestone strata underlying the wet. You will cross occasional fire lanes, and the trail will briefly follow them. At 5.3 miles, pass near a small cypress dome to the left of the trail. These forested wetlands add another ecotone to the overall Corbett nature experience.

At 6.0 miles, reach the signed spur left to Bowman Island. Here, walk south across a grassy marsh to enter more thickly vegetated habitat than any you have encountered thus far. The shady hammock has a secret hidden aura. The open space underneath the trees is limited, but a small party can squeeze a tent or two in without compromising the room to move around. Enjoy your little secret sanctuary here in the heart of big Corbett WMA.

## Mileages

| | |
|---|---|
| 0.0 | Parking area |
| 0.8 | Wetlands Bypass |
| 1.1 | Other end of Wetland Bypass |
| 6.0 | Spur to Bowman Island |
| 6.1 | Bowman Island Campsite |
| 12.2 | Parking area |

### Be Weatherwise When Backpacking

Ominous clouds rolled in overhead, darkening the March day by the moment. I was backpacking the Florida Trail in the Osceola National Forest. By now, the western sky had turned nearly black, so I pulled my weather radio out of my pack. The monotonous computer voice delivered ominous warnings of heavy storms accompanied by heavier rain and copious lightning.

I needed to find a camp—and fast! While hiking down trail I scanned each potential campsite closely, looking for signs of ponding on the ground to avoid and high spots on which to pitch my tarp.

I spotted a likely site and dropped my pack. The less-used locale offered a mound slightly higher than the surrounding terrain. Tent drainage. I pitched the tent and called it camp. Noting the potential high winds, I looked overhead for dead standing trees, known as "widow-makers" for their propensity to tumble on unsuspecting campers, then took extra care in battening down my plastic enclave, despite peals of lightning shooting sideways across the sky.

A line of strong showers rushed toward me in a low rumble. I dove into the tent and prepared for the aquatic siege. Soon, rain pelted the plastic, which flapped wildly with each punishing gust. Lightning repeatedly illuminated my shelter, followed by ground-shaking thunder loud enough to wake the dead—or at least a Florida backpacker. Next day, I found out the area had received more than 3 inches of rain! Water puddled in places, yet my judicious choice of campsites had kept me dry.

Backpackers live and die with the weather and the seasons. Reveling in the changes, we wait with anticipation as each season unfolds, along with its unique conditions, each potentially threatening in its own way—the storms of spring, the heat and lightning of summer, the first cold blasts of fall, the chill winds and temperatures of winter.

Knowing the weather when backpacking is paramount. Having an idea of what to expect allows you to bring gear and clothing appropriate for the predicted situations—or call the backpack off altogether. However, try to play the weather cards you are dealt. Avoid becoming a slave to the weather forecasts, reacting to their declarations as a servant to its master. I call it "weather paralysis," not knowing a course of action when the weather is iffy.

After all, what do you do when there's a 50 percent chance of rain?

Avoid weather paralysis, but be prepared and informed. Know the possibilities and have not only the clothing and gear contingencies covered but also alternate plans if the weather gets dangerous.

Phones can offer instant weather predictions and real-time radar, but since reception is not guaranteed, I recommend bringing a portable weather radio. They come in small backpacking sizes and weights, often with AM/FM radio bands included. Weather radio broadcasts originate from the National Oceanic and Atmospheric Administration (NOAA), with more than a thousand transmitters stretching throughout the United States. NOAA not only predicts forthcoming weather, but it also gives short-term forecasts, which can be helpful during strong, potentially life-threatening storms.

No matter what, check the weather before leaving home. Furthermore, learn weather averages well before embarking to a distant destination so you can get an idea of typical temperatures and precipitation of the area during the time you plan to backpack. That way you will be weatherwise when embarking on your adventure.

# 40

## Jonathan Dickinson Backpack

### Overview

This worthy backpack uses both the famed Ocean-to-Lake Trail and the Eagles View Multi-Use Trail System at Jonathan Dickinson State Park to fashion a backpack that tours park wildlands to first reach the pretty Kitching Creek campsites, and then the less-used Scrub Jay campsites. Both backcountry camping areas are reservable and together make an easy two-night adventure; the backpack can also be tackled as a single overnighter.

**Distance & Configuration**: 10.7-mile loop with spur to campsite
**Difficulty**: Easy
**Outstanding Features**: Kitching Creek, flatwoods views
**Scenery**: 4
**Solitude**: 2
**Family-Friendly**: 4
**Canine-Friendly**: 3
**Fees/Permits**: Fee campsites
**Best Season**: Late November through early April
**Maps**: Eagles View Multi-Use Trail System, Florida Trail in Jonathan Dickinson State Park
**For More Info**: Jonathan Dickinson State Park, 16450 SE Federal Hwy, Hobe Sound, FL 33455, 772-546-2771, https://www.floridastateparks.org/
**Finding the Trailhead**: From exit 96 on I-95 near Hobe Sound, take CR 708 East for 6.5 miles to turn right on US 1 south. Follow it for 4.6 miles to turn right into the park entrance. Get your camping permit at the ranger station and then proceed for 3 miles to the Eagles View trailhead on your right. GPS trailhead coordinates: 27.006005, -80.142058

Coming in at 10,500 acres, Jonathan Dickinson State Park boasts an expansive trail system, including a section of the Ocean-to-Lake Trail linking Lake Okeechobee to the Atlantic Ocean, as well as the Eagles View Multi-Use

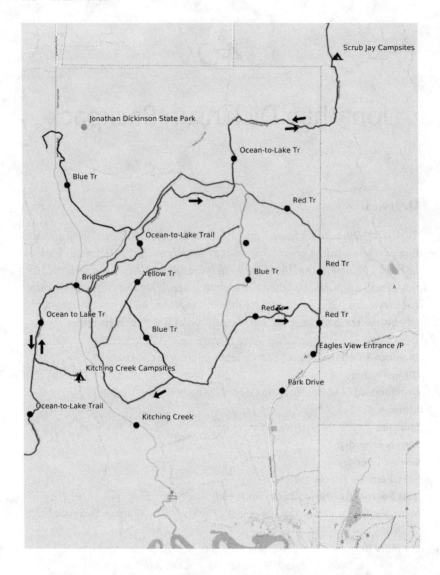

Trail System and still other pathways. Habitats in the preserve range from semi-tropical hammocks along the Loxahatchee—one of Florida's two federally designated wild and scenic rivers—to pine flatwoods to rare coastal sandhills. The popular park also features varied camping opportunities, including two designated backcountry campsites that contrast one another, expanding the backpacking experience at Jonathan Dickinson.

Kitching Creek is the more popular of the two camping areas. It is offers three specific campsites set in a palm-pine grove. Each campsite features a picnic table and fire ring. A pump well and privy are available for Kitching

Bridging blackwater Kitching Creek.

Creek campers. Scrub Jay Camp is set in tall pines over grasses bordered by scrub. The widespread trees give partial shade to the sites, each with picnic table and benches. A pump well and privy serve the Scrub Jay Camp as well. An additional trailside seating area is located near the Scrub Jay privy. Call ahead to make campsite reservations.

The trails at Jonathan Dickinson State are well-marked, -signed, and -maintained. Numbered posts mark most trail intersections of the Eagles View Multi-Use Trail System, shared by hikers, bicyclers, and equestrians, though hikers dominate in numbers. Unmarked fire roads also course through the park. Ignore all sand roads unless signed. Much of the hike traverses double-tracks that wander through flatwoods broken by cypress swamp strands. Under normal winter hiking conditions, you should be able to keep your feet dry for the entire adventure. With your back to the park road, leave right from the Eagles View parking area, heading north along a double-track. Keep north along a power-line clearing, working across a cypress strand, where these moisture-tolerant trees grow along stream drainages. At 0.2 mile, trail junction 1, split left with the Red Trail, westbound on a double-track through slash pines with a wiregrass, gallberry, and palmetto understory, as well as wax myrtle. Cypress domes pock the pine forest in the distance.

At 0.9 mile, trail junction 7, intersect the Blue Trail, which will be your return route. For now, keep straight on the Red Trail, with nothing but you, wildlife, and the wind blowing through the pines. Ignore unblazed sand roads, and at 1.3 miles at trail junction 6, a second Blue Trail splits right. Stay with the Red Trail, coming within sight of Kitching Creek's lush woods and then turning right, north, keeping Kitching Creek off to your left.

At 2.1 miles, at trail junction 5, keep straight as the Yellow Trail comes in on your right, still running parallel to the live oak rich woods of Kitching Creek. At 2.4 miles, meet the orange-blazed, hiker-only, Ocean-to-Lake Trail. Head left to soon reach a hiker bridge over 10-foot-wide Kitching Creek flowing under a shady canopy of oaks and palms, clotted with coco plum, ferns, and orchids, bridging a second stream before popping back out to pine flatwoods. Stay with the Ocean-to-Lake Trail, turning south to meet the spur to Kitching Creek Camp at 3.1 miles. Head left here, reaching thicker woods and the campsites at 3.3 miles. Site 1 is shaded and to your left. Site 2, with pines and palms, is the most popular. Site 3 offers more solitude in pine and scrub but is more open. The pump well is near Site 1. Recommended sites in order are 2,1, then 3.

Backtrack to the east side of Kitching Creek, keeping north on the Ocean-to-Lake Trail at 4.4 miles. Continue northwesterly on single-track in pines but working around wet depression ponds. At 5.7 miles, cross the Red Trail, staying north. Stick with Ocean-to-Lake Trail blazes as the single-track goes on and off old roadbeds. Enjoy the long-ranging parkland views. At 6.1 miles, curve east, working past some ponds to cross back under massive power lines at 6.6 miles. Stay with the orange blazes and at 7.1 miles, reach a privy and benches and a fire ring. This is sometimes confused with the Scrub Jay campsites because of the benches here. Stay with the Ocean-to-Lake Trail, passing the pump well for the camp and then splitting right to the official Scrub Jay camps, located on a slight slope among widespread pines, at 7.2 miles. Site 1 is more open, and Site 2 offers a little more shade.

Next day, backtrack on the Ocean-to-Lake Trail for 1.5 miles, then go left, easterly, on the Red Trail, picking up new pathway. The double-track is easy in pine flatwoods. At 8.8 miles at trail junction 3, split right, southbound on the Blue Trail. Just ahead, the Yellow Trail splits right, and you stay with the Blue Trail southbound, returning to trail junction 7 at 9.8 miles. From here it is a simple 0.9 mile backtrack to the Eagles View trailhead, completing the fun South Florida backpack.

## Mileages

0.0     Eagles View trailhead
2.4     Left on Ocean-to-Lake Trail
3.3     Kitching Creek Campsites
7.2     Scrub Jay Campsites
10.7    Eagles View trailhead

# ACKNOWLEDGMENTS

Thanks to all the trail blazers, trail maintainers, backpacking clubs, and all the folks who keep the pathways coursing through the Sunshine State so backpackers like us can enjoy them. Thanks also to all who have joined me on the trail, backpacking in Florida, especially my wife, Keri Anne.

JOHNNY MOLLOY is a writer and adventurer based in Johnson City, Tennessee. His outdoor passion ignited on a backpacking trip in Great Smoky Mountains National Park. That first foray unleashed a love of the outdoors that led Johnny to spend over 4,000 nights backpacking, canoe camping and tent camping throughout North America over the past four decades.

Friends enjoyed his outdoor adventure stories; one even suggested he write a book. He pursued his friend's idea and soon parlayed his love of the outdoors into an occupation. The results of his efforts are over 80 books and guides, most of them in multiple editions, written for 6 different publishers. His writings include how-to outdoor guides and true adventure stories, as well as hiking, camping and paddling books covering all or parts of 28 states.

Though primarily involved with book publications, Molloy also writes for varied magazines and websites. To this day, he continues writing and traveling extensively throughout the United States, endeavoring in a variety of outdoor pursuits.

A Christian, Johnny is an active member of Christ Community Church and Gideons International. His non-outdoor interests include reading, American history and University of Tennessee sports. For the latest on Johnny, please visit www.johnnymolloy.com.